THERE IS A YOUNG ECCENTRIC LOOSE
IN THE MAJOR LEAGUES.

HE LOOKS LIKE A CROSS BETWEEN HARPO MARX
AND AN OSTRICH.

HE PITCHES
LIKE A WHIRLWIND WITH ARMS.

HE'S THE BEST THING TO HIT DETROIT
SINCE THE ASSEMBLY LINE.

AND THE BEST THING THAT'S HAPPENED TO
BASEBALL SINCE THE NIGHT GAME!

HE'S
MARK (THE BIRD) FIDRYCH
AND
<u>GO BIRD GO!</u>
IS THE FANTASTIC STORY OF HIS METEORIC RISE
TO THE TOP OF AMERICA'S FAVORITE SPORT!

THE MOST THRILLING SPORTS STORY OF THIS—
OR ANY—SEASON!

Go Bird Go!

by
JIM BENAGH
and
JIM HAWKINS

A DELL BOOK

Published by
Dell Publishing Co., Inc.
1 Dag Hammarskjold Plaza
New York, New York 10017

Dell ® TM 681510, Dell Publishing Co., Inc.
Printed in the United States of America

First printing—August 1976

To Leslie and Mark,
who are every bit as rare as The Bird.

J.H.

And to Jeffrey and Jason,
who can be as much fun.

J.B.

Contents

Go Bird Go!

Prologue

It's a bird. It's a plane. It's Superm—!

No, it's a bird after all.

The Bird, to be exact. The one and only.

Even Superman would have a difficult time following Mark (The Bird) Fidrych's act.

The Bird swooped down out of nowhere in 1976, stole the game of baseball away from the mercenaries, who considered it merely a business, and gave it back to the fans.

Thousands of men have played major-league baseball in the past century. Hundreds of them have been heralded as heroes. But no one has ever turned the fans on like this twenty-one-year-old Detroit Tiger rookie. It's his ball, his game, his fans.

"If somebody told you to write a script about a young ballplayer," said Tiger General Manager Jim Campbell, "and you wrote what has happened to Mark Fidrych, nobody would believe it. They'd lock you up."

"Go, Bird, Go!"

It wasn't a baseball game, it was a happening. Fifty thousand delirious fans, in a frenzy, all turned on by a gangling kid with long curly hair.

Baseball is the medium Mark Fidrych used. Other than pumping gas and fixing cars, throwing a ball is the only professional skill he possessed. But he had gotten through to them—to the more than 50,000 fans in the stands—and to thousands of others who couldn't fit into Tiger Stadium on July 3, 1976.

Aside from the usual fireworks earlier in the week, Detroit, Michigan, didn't have much of a celebration planned for America's 200th birthday. In fact, this particular game between the Detroit Tigers and the Baltimore Orioles was billed as "Windsor Night," a salute to the Canadian city directly across the Detroit River.

But, of all the birthday celebrations across America, this unplanned one took the cake. Fifty thousand Americans were lifting their beers and cokes to toast America's greatest resource—as the saying goes—youth. One youth in particular: The Bird.

"Go, Bird, Go!"

How many times can 50,000 people scream it? How many times can they leap to their feet to applaud one person? How much adulation can they heap on a rookie pitcher with an 8–1 record?

How much?

"The Bird Is the Word," said the orange and black buttons that hundreds of fans had purchased from hawkers outside the stadium. Others wore "Bird" T-shirts, purchased from an enterprising peddler in a pickup truck. In the stands, youngsters strolled through the aisles carrying signs hastily drawn on bedsheets. One sign told it all. "Mark, We Love You!" it read.

Baseball crowds don't normally show up until about half an hour before a game. Only the connoisseurs get there early enough to watch batting and fielding practice. Nobody ever comes to watch the pitcher warm up.

But this night the stands began to fill as soon as the gates opened at six o'clock for the eight o'clock game. Long lines of people had been stretched along Al Kaline and Mickey Cochrane drives, outside the stadium, for more than two hours before that. And there would still be a crowd outside the ballpark after the game began, as thousands of fans showed up, only to discover there were no tickets left.

Detroit was a joyous city that night.

At Metropolitan Airport, a white-haired lady in her seventies was patiently trying to explain to her friend from New York how Mark Fidrych smoothed the dirt on the pitching mound with his hand. At the Lindell AC, Detroit's most popular post-game drinking spot, the fans who had been unable to buy tickets to the ballgame congregated to commiserate and talk about The Bird.

All week long, "The Bird" had been "the word" in Detroit. Ever since Fidrych defeated the New York Yankees the previous Monday in front of a full house and a national television audience, fans and folks who never cared much about baseball had been looking forward to this game.

A Michigan state legislator introduced a resolution asking the Tigers to raise Mark's salary, which was at the major league's bare minimum. A radio listener proposed that Fidrych be named the official state bird of Michigan, replacing the robin. A suburban couple named their newborn son Mark Fidrych.

Few in Detroit were talking about the Bicentennial. Almost everyone was talking about The Bird.

After all, a Bicentennial comes along every two hundred years. But The Bird was one of a kind.

Normally, the Detroit-Baltimore game would

have drawn between 20,000 and 25,000 fans. The Tigers were going nowhere in the standings, and the Orioles were chasing them.

There was only one reason for 50,000 people to be at the ballpark: The Bird.

Originally, Fidrych had been scheduled to pitch the night before in Baltimore. And about 30,000 fans in that Maryland city bought tickets for the game, assuming they were going to get to see the suddenly famous Tiger pitcher. A Detroit television station, in an unprecedented move, rearranged its prime time schedule in order to broadcast the game back to Michigan because of the incredible interest in Fidrych.

Then, when the Tigers were rained out on Wednesday night, Detroit manager Ralph Houk had to push all his pitchers back a day, which meant Fidrych wouldn't work until the Tigers returned home to host the Orioles Saturday night. The television station immediately cancelled all plans to carry the game in Baltimore.

And when the ticket windows at Tiger Stadium opened the next morning, the fans were lined up waiting to buy tickets for Saturday night.

All because of The Bird.

Here was a twenty-one-year-old ballplayer who had completely captivated baseball, both in Detroit and across the country. The two major television networks that broadcast big-league baseball nationally—NBC and ABC—were begging Ralph Houk to change his pitching rotation so they could feature him. Owners of the other eleven American League teams were in constant contact with the Tigers, checking to see if and when Fidrych might fill their ballparks. Professional agents were drooling at the thought of representing him.

Why The Bird? Why this kid, who was certainly no Sandy Koufax when it came to pitching, a third-year professional who wasn't even expected to make the Tigers big-league team a few months before, a pitcher who didn't get his first major-league starting assignment until he had been with the team for five weeks?

There was an aura of mystery about the power he held over his followers.

Mark Fidrych, a skinny, six-foot three-inch kid with long hair and a loose lease on life, was a symbol of the seventies. He was one of those kids adults didn't like in the sixties, but had now come to accept; even dads wore long hair now, and mothers wore faded jeans.

They could look at this symbol of youth, eye to eye—they didn't have to look down at him. Now they could enjoy him.

Jimmy Butsicaris, the owner of the Lindell AC, who has seen athletes—and their female followers —come and go at his pub for many years, tried to explain why there were so many little old ladies among the clusters of Fidrych's newly found fans.

"He's everybody's son," Jimmy said. "People are used to that kind of kid now."

Fidrych's irreverent attitude toward major-league baseball made it seem like a game again.

And when he pitched, he put his whole body into winning. His arms flailed, his body shook, he aimed the ball at the plate like a dart, and he talked to himself—and to the ball—while he pitched.

That was what really turned people on at first— the fact that he talked to the baseball. He really talked to it.

"Get the *bleep* down . . . get the *bleep* down," he would say whenever the ball wandered higher than the batter's knees.

"Come on now, curve . . . we gotta curve."

Most of the time, though, Fidrych just talked to himself.

"Get it over . . . come on now, get it the *bleep* over. . . . I gotta throw hard . . . I gotta throw hard. . . . Let it flow . . . let it flow. . . . You got the motion. . . . Slow the body and let it fly.

"Sometimes I'll look at the ball and say, 'Look, ball, we've got to do this or we've got to do that,'" he admitted. "But I'm really just reminding myself what to do. It's just my way of keeping my head together and keeping my concentration on where to release the ball.

"You gotta be able to keep your mind together. It's hard to keep your mind together sometimes, but you have to do it. You can't lose your mind. Because when you lose your mind, the ball is lost."

And the more The Bird talked, the more they loved him.

There were other reasons, too.

The working man could identify with him. He was making $16,000 a year, like a lot of them.

Unlike baseball's new breed—and sports' new breed—he wasn't trying to shake down the Tigers for more money. In the same week when Baseball Commissioner Bowie Kuhn and Oakland A's owner Charley Finley were battling over million-dollar ballplayers, Fidrych was telling reporters:

"I don't need an agent. Only I know my true value and can negotiate it."

And he didn't ask for a penny more, although he did receive an additional $7,500 bonus that had been written into his contract when he had originally signed, right out of high school. But the Tigers would have owed him that even if he had been 1–8.

There may have been other factors that made him a hit in Detroit, too.

The city was crying for a hero. Crime, and the fear of crime, had Detroiters longing for something, someone, to divert their attention.

In Mark Fidrych they found something they could think about, talk about, and, for a few hours each week, become totally absorbed with.

Detroit is a great baseball town. The fans there have always worshiped their heroes—from Ty Cobb and Mickey Cochrane and Hank Greenberg to Al Kaline and Willie Horton and Denny McLain.

But this was something different.

It was more than loyal fans showering their favorite player on their favorite team with attention and affection.

The Bird was bigger than that.

Maybe, for the moment, even bigger than base-ball.

Saturday, May 15
VS. CLEVELAND

A light rain was falling on Detroit when The Bird left his modest suburban apartment, and the forecast called for more. If there was one day in his life when he wished it wouldn't rain, this had to be it.

After five weeks of sitting in the dugout, doing nothing more than leading the cheers for his teammates, Fidrych was finally going to get a chance to pitch. To start. To prove what he could do.

He was keyed up. He couldn't wait for his little Dodge Colt to get him to the ballpark. This was something very special.

So special that he thought of inviting his father to fly in from Boston to watch him pitch. But, with the threatening weather he decided against it. His family had made one futile trip to Detroit, driving all the way to watch him sit on the bench. He didn't want to put them through that again.

The Bird had been scheduled to make his first major-league start a week before. But the Tigers were rained out of a doubleheader in Chicago just prior to that, and Manager Houk was forced to juggle his starting rotation. Fidrych, therefore, was passed over for the moment in favor of Houk's tested veterans.

Now Houk needed him again. Because the schedule had become crowded with games, the Tigers were going to employ five starting pitchers instead of the usual four—and Mark Fidrych was Houk's choice as the fifth man in the pecking order. His first game would be against the Cleveland Indians.

As Fidrych pulled into the players' parking area at Tiger Stadium that Saturday morning, the streets were deserted. There were no cars jamming the streets, bumper to bumper, searching for parking spaces and a chance to get inside to watch The Bird warm up. There were no pins, no bumper stickers, no T-shirts, no hint that The Bird even existed.

The ticket booths were just as quiet. Extra help wouldn't be needed this day.

It was just a dreary mid-May afternoon—the kind of day that inspires people to stay home and watch television instead of seeing the show live at the ballpark.

After all, who was Mark Fidrych? Most of the 14,583 fans could not even pronounce the rookie's name. They heard it right—"Fid'-rich"—when the public-address announcer introduced him to them.

They had a chance to practice it while they sat through a twenty-six-minute rain delay.

Fidrych fidgeted, he worried, and he was saddened at the sight of that rain, even though it was little more than a drizzle. But he was so worked up he would have been happy to pitch in a thundershower.

As it was, the drizzle did continue, and Fidrych pitched miracles in it. And an hour and fifty-seven minutes after he first took the mound, he was no longer a total stranger to hundreds of thousands of baseball fans, many as far away as California.

Mark Fidrych had come close to pitching a no-hitter in his major-league debut as a starter. Along with the witnesses in the stands, he had two other audiences—the Tigers' own statewide television network and NBC's back-up national "Game of the Week."

For six straight innings, those fans sat in awe as Fidrych held the Indians hitless and helpless, threatening to become only the fourth pitcher in more than a hundred years of major-league baseball to throw a no-hitter in his first start.

Along the way, he was talking to the ball . . . talking to himself . . . pointing and aiming the ball at the plate before he threw—anything to get that ball to go where he wanted it to go.

His pitching coach, Fred Gladding, was baffled, even though he knew more about this hyped-up rookie than most. He had been hoping for Fidrych to last five or six innings, then they could bring in a relief pitcher.

But to expect all this—a near no-hitter coupled with those funny mannerisms that were turning on the crowd—it was too much.

At the start of each inning, he would stoop over and smooth out the damp dirt on the mound with his left hand. In the sixth inning, when the grounds crew attempted to make some minor repairs on the field, Fidrych refused to let them anywhere near the mound. Instead, he grabbed a handful of sand from their wheelbarrow and galloped back to the mound, where he personally patted it in place.

"When I'm pitching, the mound belongs to me," he would say later, and say often during the season as each new wave of reporters inquired about it for the first time. His funny little antics in preparing the mound as no one in the history of baseball had done before became his most famous trademark. Yet he was doing it for a purpose, not for show.

The first fourteen Cleveland batters who attempted to hit his pitches failed. They all went out. In fact, only one of those fourteen could even push a ball past the infield.

Though there's an unwritten rule in baseball that your teammates don't say anything when you have a no-hitter going, Fidrych admitted later he knew what was happening.

In fact, when the fifteenth Indian batter to face

him, Alan Ashby, was walked, Fidrych told himself, "There goes my perfect game."

Two innings later, Cleveland's Buddy Bell bounced a ball toward left field that hopped under third-baseman Aurelio Rodriguez's glove. It was a clean single, and Fidrych lost his chance for no-hit fame.

"Well, you lost the no-hitter, but you've still got a shutout," Fidrych told himself.

Moments later, that disappeared, too. Cleveland's Rick Manning slammed a base hit up the middle, sending Bell to third. Bell soon scored when Rico Carty's high hopping grounder to second-baseman Gary Sutherland gave him running room.

"Now all you got left is the win, and you'd better get it," Fidrych told Fidrych.

Fidrych listened. He retired the next eight Indians without a struggle. He won, 2–1, giving up only two hits in the process.

Few pitchers in the long history of the game had ever done much better. Alva (Bobo) Holloman of the old St. Louis Browns held the Philadelphia Athletics hitless in his first start twenty-three years before. Two other major-league hurlers before the turn of the century also threw no-hitters their first times out.

Four other pitchers had one-hitters in their first attempts at pitching in the majors.

Other rookies, like Bill Slayback of the Tigers, got off to brilliant starts but cloudy finishes. Slayback had a seven-inning no-hitter going for him, also in 1972, but he needed relief help to enable him to win the game after the no-hitter was lost.

No wonder Fidrych was excited.

It was hard to believe.

It was hard for others to believe, too—not just the brilliantly pitched game, but the antics that surrounded those well-aimed pitches.

The umpire behind the plate, Marty Springstead, admitted that if his colleague, Dale Ford, hadn't forewarned him about the Tigers' strange bird, he probably would have kicked Fidrych out of the game. Springstead said later:

"It was lucky Ford told me about him because I would have thought he was yelling at me when he started all the talking on the mound. Ford had him in the minors [in 1975] and he was going to run him, too. But the kid's manager came out and told Ford, 'He's not yelling at you.'

"When an umpire sees a guy out there talking like that, you think he's cursing you. But this kid is different. He's a strange boy."

The conquered Indians were less ready to give Fidrych the benefit of the doubt.

"It was one of those days when everything went his way," said Rico Carty, a well-traveled veteran who had faced many strange situations in his long big-league career, but nothing like this. "He just psyched us out with all the stuff he did on the mound.

"The more he did it, the more you wanted to hit him. My mind was more on what he was doing than on my hitting. In our dugout everyone was saying, 'Let's get that guy.' But we were too concerned about that and didn't pay enough attention to our hitting. Once you start paying attention to him, you get all tied up.

"I've never seen anything like it. Sometimes I was almost laughing. How can you hit when you're laughing?

"The first time I got up, he pointed the ball at me, and I said to myself, 'What the hell is he doing and saying?' It was like he was trying to hypnotize us.

"I just said, 'Throw the ball.'

"Then he did—and I couldn't hit it."

Alan Ashby, Carty's teammate, said that after a while he resorted to talking to his bat in order to try to get a hit off Fidrych.

"I said, 'Okay, you're gonna get a hit, you're gonna get a hit.' I thought his antics were just a passing thing. But that's really him."

Another Cleveland player, Buddy Bell, said, "He really messes up your concentration. He's always talking to himself—even up until he's getting ready to throw. All you could hear was, 'Okay, ball, we're going to do this or do that.'"

At least one of the Indians saw a little humor in it all, however.

Right-fielder John Lowenstein vowed that the next time he faced Fidrych he was going to call time and ask the umpire to inspect the ball. Then he said he would grab the ball, hold it to his ear, and listen to what The Bird had told it.

Already that first afternoon it was obvious there never had been another pitcher like The Bird.

Except for those who knew him in high school or the minors—where the "crowds" rarely reached 2,000—The Bird had gone public for the first time. You can't get a better showcase for the off-beat than major-league baseball. There, the crowds, the sportswriters, the television people will grab at anything that turns them on, especially when it's as new and different as Fidrych had been this Saturday in mid-May.

But The Bird wasn't exactly new to the Tigers themselves. They had had the sneak preview, having watched him pitch briefly in two other games —and having heard all those weird stories that had been passed up from the minor leagues.

Ralph Houk had brought him out of the bullpen for a relief stint in the bottom of the ninth inning against Oakland on April 20. That was his first major-league appearance.

Fidrych didn't have a chance to show his stuff.

He made two pitches, the second of which Oakland's Don Baylor drilled for a single that won the game. (Fidrych didn't get the loss because another pitcher had put the winning run on base.)

It was enough to send most youngsters into a fit of depression. But not The Bird.

When Fidrych encountered Baylor on the field during hitting practice the next night, he boldly informed him, "Everybody gets a lucky hit once in a while."

Baylor couldn't believe his ears.

"I told him he ought to wait until he's been around here for a while before he starts talking like that," said the veteran player.

Weeks later, when the incident was recalled, Fidrych could not even remember facing Baylor. That's how much of an impression that hit made on him.

Fidrych also had pitched an inning of relief against the Minnesota Twins on May 5, and that, too, was lackluster.

But the Tigers did not have him in the major leagues to pitch in the bullpen.

"We were figuring on him as our fifth starter," Houk explained. "But with all the off-days in April, we didn't need a fifth starter until early May. Then we had those rainouts, so we didn't need him then either. But we were counting on him all along."

Instead of starting, Fidrych regularly threw along the sidelines, shagged fly balls and ran in the outfield to keep in shape, and cheered his teammates during games from the dugout with his incessant, shrieking chatter.

"He was always working on stuff," said pitching coach Fred Gladding. "I'd get to the park and he'd say, 'Come on, let's go, hit me some grounders.' And we'd go out and I'd hit ground balls back to the mound for fifteen minutes. He improved quite a bit in that area."

When the Tiger pitchers would sprint up and down the outfield, Fidrych would run faster and longer than anyone.

He thrived on work.

Then came the win over Cleveland, at a time when the Tigers were in need of a few victories.

"For a kid—a rookie—he pitched a helluva game," said Gladding. "I couldn't believe it. He pitched fantastic."

Houk, a veteran of twenty-five years in major-league baseball, said he couldn't remember a pitcher ever doing a better job than Fidrych in his first start.

"I really didn't know what to expect from him," Houk said. "You are never sure in a situation like that. The amazing thing was that he was as strong at the end of the game as he was at the start."

Houk, who had managed two last-place teams in Detroit, said he was especially impressed with Fidrych's enthusiasm.

"Everybody in the park throws every pitch with this kid," the manager said. "But he's far from being whacky. That's not a flake out there on the mound. The things he does are just a nervous reaction."

Everybody in the Tiger organization made it clear that no one had ever tried to get Fidrych to change his act.

And after that opening victory, none of them would dare.

"I gotta get high to pitch," The Bird said. "I gotta psyche myself up. I gotta be wild. When I'm relaxed, when I'm not talking to the ball, I find I do badly."

When the first game was recorded, and the word about The Bird began to spread across the country, the pitcher himself tried to put it all into perspective.

It's safe to say he didn't really realize what he had accomplished, or how he had grabbed the public spotlight. He described his happiness in much simpler terms.

"I couldn't ask for anything better than just being in the big leagues," he said.

"Damn, up here I've got more spikes than I know what to do with. I didn't even have to buy them. The same with my gloves. It's great.

"You know what's really neat about being in the big leagues? It's going and seeing all those good fields, especially the stadiums. In high school I played on fields that had weeds in the infield. And in the minors I saw some fields that were kept up and some that weren't.

"Here they cut the weeds. It's neat to see fields that are kept up like that."

The Bird wasn't finished talking.

"Getting to the big leagues makes me feel like I've accomplished what I wanted. I wasn't good in school, and baseball is the place where I can do good.

"I want to be good. If you pitch and get a 'W,' that's good. If you get an 'L,' that's bad."

For Fidrych, it was still all as simple as that.

GAME PLAYED MAY 15

CLEVELAND	ab	r	h	bi	DETROIT	ab	r	h	bi
Lowenstin rf	4	0	0	0	LeFlore cf	4	1	2	0
BBell 3b	4	1	1	0	AJohnson lf	4	0	1	0
Manning cf	4	0	1	0	Horton dh	2	0	1	1
Carty dh	3	0	0	1	Staub rf	3	0	1	0
Hendrick lf	3	0	0	0	JThompson 1b	3	1	1	0
Ashby c	2	0	0	0	ARodriguez 3b	2	0	0	0
Howard 1b	3	0	0	0	Veryzer ss	2	0	0	1
Kuiper 2b	3	0	0	0	Sutherland 2b	3	0	0	0
Duffy ss	3	0	0	0	Kimm c	3	0	1	0
PDobson p	0	0	0	0	Fidrych p	0	0	0	0
Total	29	1	2	1	Total	26	2	7	2

CLEVELAND .... 000 000 100—1
DETROIT .... 100 100 00x—2

E—B.Bell. DP—Cleveland 2. LOB—Cleveland 2, Detroit 3.
2B—J.Thompson. SB—Kimm, Manning. S—A.Rodriguez. SF—
Horton, Veryzer.

	IP	H	R	ER	BB	SO
P.Dobson (L, 3—4)	8	7	2	2	0	2
Fidrych (W, 1—0)	9	2	1	1	1	5

T—1:57. A—14, 583.

Tuesday, May 25
AT BOSTON

A small crowd was waiting for Mark Fidrych in the Boston airport when the Tigers flew in from Baltimore. Most of them were family or friends. They were there to greet Mark—or Markie, as his mother called him—Fidrych, the outstanding rookie with a 1–0 record during his major-league career.

Boston's Fenway Park is located just about forty-five minutes from Northboro, Massachusetts, where Fidrych grew up.

But Fenway could hardly be called familiar terrain for The Bird, who would be making his second big-league start. By his own count, Fidrych would be entering that ballpark for only the third or fourth time. His mother said he just couldn't sit still long enough to watch a game, and that he would rather be playing than watching anyway.

Fidrych also said he never bought a copy of *The Sporting News,* the weekly paper that serves as a trade journal for professional players. The reason was simple: He never was a fan.

Maybe it was a good thing that Mark knew so little about the Red Sox and their tightly enclosed ballpark, which pitchers have historically found to be home-run prone. The Red Sox, who designed their teams to take advantage of the short fences, were loaded with power hitters who had carried the team all the way to the seventh game of the World Series in 1975.

With two busloads of Northboro fans in the stands to cheer him on, Mark pitched well enough to win. He was talking like mad to the ball, and apparently telling it the right things. Despite a case of pre-game butterflies, he got off to a fine start. He pitched three shutout innings.

Then in the fourth, he walked Boston catcher Carlton Fisk. The next man up, Carl Yastrzemski, slammed a home run—a long shot that carried above the left-field wall and into a screen that towers above it. The Bird knew that he had thrown a bad pitch, high and outside, when he wanted it down and inside.

That homer gave the Red Sox a 2–0 lead, and there was only one thing to do—bear down. He did.

Unfortunately, the Tigers were mired in a bad slump. The hitters, except for Ron LeFlore, who was batting .402 and had a twenty-seven-game hitting streak, were not producing.

This day the batters would offer little support. The Tigers got only seven hits off Red Sox ace Luis Tiant, and only LeFlore's double went for extra bases. There wasn't even a threat of a score as Tiant put down the last eight batters he faced.

But The Bird put on a pretty good show of his own after giving up the homer to Yastrzemski. He allowed only one additional single.

When Yastrzemski, who hit three homers in a single game against the Tigers earlier in Detroit, got to bat again, Fidrych was determined to cool him off.

He was even more determined when "Yaz" disturbed him by making a hefty, crowd-pleasing swing at his first pitch. "He was going to show everybody he got a homer off me and how he was going to do it again," said The Bird.

Fidrych said later that Yastrzemski was just showing off. Perturbed, The Bird thought seriously of sending a pitch across Yastrzemski's chest to teach him a lesson—to teach a lesson to a former Most Valuable Player who was in the major leagues before Fidrych reached the first grade.

But The Bird changed his mind and threw the same pitch he had wanted to throw the first time, when Yastrzemski had slammed the homer. This time he threw it right and got Yastrzemski on a ground ball.

The game finished 2–0 Boston, an uneventful day for The Bird except that his parents got to see him play. And he had won a spot for sure in Manager Ralph Houk's pitching rotation.

* * *

Mark Steven Fidrych was born August 14, 1954, in Worcester, Massachusetts, but grew up in nearby Northboro, population 9,218.

Things happened so fast at the start of his baseball career that journalists sometimes reported he was a native of Worcester. The Bird corrected them: "I haven't lived there since I left the hospital." He said it with a straight face.

He was a second child, with one older sister and two younger ones. His grandparents on his father's side were Polish, which hasn't hurt in Detroit with its large Polish population, and his parents on his mother's side were Danish.

Being an only son, he is very close to his mother, who calls him Markie. He, in turn, in his letters to her, addresses her as Mother Fidrych, and sends her roses on her birthday.

She has a wealth of childhood stories about Mark and tells them freely. One of her favorites is about the time when he was three and got lost at the shopping center. She found him in the front window of a Sears, Roebuck store, marking perhaps the first time he was showcased.

His dad, Paul, was a good athlete who especially enjoyed bowling, and got Mark interested in sports when he was very young. In fact, Mark's first appearance on television was on a bowling show when he was still a little boy.

By four or five, Mark was already interested in baseball. Interested so much, his mother said, that he had a nightly ritual of not letting her tuck him in bed until he put his glove under his mattress. After his kiss goodnight, he would pull the beak of his baseball cap over his eyes and go to sleep.

"There's always been excitement around him," said his father, who is not as outgoing as his wife, Virginia, but just as proud of their son.

Paul Fidrych remembered such things as Mark rolling down a hill into a fire—he didn't get hurt—and bouncing an acorn into a teacher's coffee cup by accident.

When he visited home during the Tigers' trip to Boston, he put a boat in the water with a friend—but forgot to put the plug in it. Since he had only one suit with him, and was wearing it until it got muddy when the boat sank, he had to come home in the next-to-nothing.

Mark walked into the house wearing what amounted to a loin cloth, which prompted youngest sister, Lorie, age eleven, to announce: "Hey, everybody, here's Adam."

Mark's boyhood interests were the normal ones—sports, playing pool, tinkering with cars, working in the gas station, girls, etc. Later he learned to cook and now specializes in dishes like golapki, a Polish meal featuring stuffed cabbage.

And, yes, his mother said, even in his teens he did spend a lot of time watching *Sesame Street*, though no one thought to nickname him Bird until he joined his first professional team.

The family is middle class. Paul Fidrych taught school, then became an assistant principal at a junior high in Worcester. So it was almost natural that he would get his son started in a sport like baseball.

Mark was good in Little League baseball. There were some who felt he should have been with the varsity in his first year at Algonquin High School, where he also played some football and basketball. But he wasn't moved up from the jayvee team that freshman year.

After the nondescript start at Algonquin, Mark decided to try out for the local American Legion team in the summer of 1971. Legion ball was the natural progression in the summer for a teenager from the Little Leagues and Pony Leagues.

The manager of Picard Post 234 in Northboro, Ted Rolfe, remembers the gangling sixteen-year-old with shaggy hair asking him for a chance to pitch.

Rolfe sent him out to pitch batting practice, which was the way he tuned up all of his pitchers. He felt he could tell more by doing this than just watching a youngster throw to a catcher.

"The first pitch he threw, I just turned to one of my players and said, 'My God, where has that kid been'," recalled Rolfe, who had handled Legion players for about fifteen years. "He threw a hard, low strike that blew into the plate.

"Then I learned he had a battle with the high school coach over hair. That's why I hadn't seen him before."

Shortly after the Northboro Legion team opened its season, Fidrych got his first start.

Against a solid, poised team from Fitchburg,

Massachusetts, Fid—as he was nicknamed then—made his debut a memorable one. He pitched a no-hitter.

Displaying the same control he has now, Fidrych allowed only two men to get on base (by walks) and struck out fourteen batters.

Rolfe knew he had a gem on his hands.

Mark was a spirited player who cheered his teammates for their good plays and consoled them for their mistakes. He didn't just acknowledge those good plays, either. He rushed up to them and let them know it, even if they were in the outfield. They, in turn, responded by playing even better when he was on the mound.

"He was a real good pitcher then, right from the start," said Rolfe, who managed for fun after working for the State Employment Agency during the day. Rolfe had him for three years in the Legion program, which is a spawning ground for many future major leaguers. (In 1975, the Legion graduate of the year was Fred Lynn, who, as a rookie, also was the American League's Most Valuable Player after leading the Boston Red Sox into the World Series.)

"Unlike that first game, he was never the super strikeout pitcher, though he was very fast," said Rolfe. "But he always had the game under control. He did all the things he does now to concentrate. He'd go through a whole season of talking to the ball, but we didn't think anything of it."

Crowds of 1,500 to 1,700 would show up to watch him pitch against top teams such as Framingham and Milford and other nearby towns.

In three years, he won sixteen games and lost only three, and Rolfe said one of those defeats—a 2–0 loss to heated rival Milford—may have been his best game. It was played the morning of July 4, 1972, and Fidrych gave up only two hits while the Milford pitcher gave up one.

Rolfe recalled that Fidrych had an earned-run average of about 0.55 or 0.60. He doesn't remember him ever giving up a home run.

The tighter the situation was, the better Mark was.

There was a game in 1972 against Auburn's Legion team when Mark was protecting a 3–2 lead in the eighth inning. A man was on second when the Auburn batter sent a shot screaming out to center field. The Northboro outfielder made a great play, and Fidrych raced to the plate to back up his catcher, Bruce Morgan, while the fielder made the long throw home to get the runner, who was trying to score from second.

As the ball sailed home, the Auburn base runner came sliding in with his spikes high, intent on doing some damage to Morgan, a squat youngster with a broad chest, Morgan tagged him, ending the inning, but a fight erupted.

When Mark moved in to intervene, he caught a punch in the head that left him dizzy. After Northboro batted, there was some question whether he would be able to pitch. Rolfe saw that he was still groggy while he was warming up, so he went to the mound to check him out.

Fidrych begged for a chance to continue. Rolfe had his reservations, partly because the heart of the Auburn batting order was coming up. But he gave in.

In that ninth inning, Morgan kept feeding Mark the sign for strikes down the middle—one finger to the ground. Mark pitched nine straight of them—all perfect strikes—and retired the side.

"He was a free spirit. He did what he wanted, but he never caused any trouble," said Rolfe.

The closest there was to a problem came in a game against Framingham in 1972. Fidrych was getting beat, and eventually lost, 2–1, as a big, older man taunted him for the entire game. The fan was clearly getting on Fidrych's nerves, and affecting his concentration.

When the game was over, the Northboro team was gathering its equipment and stuffing it into duffel bags when one of the players pointed out to Rolfe that Mark was headed for the stands to have some words with his obnoxious detractor.

Rolfe cringed. But before he could do anything, Mark was on his way back to the bench. The fan sat there speechless, perhaps happy that Mark had not taken his head off.

"What did you say to him?" the manager asked, relieved that a confrontation had not taken place.

"I handed him the ball and told him he needed it more than I did," said Fidrych.

As Fidrych's feats became known, more and more scouts began showing up at Northboro Legion games. According to Rolfe, the Boston Red

Sox sent their bird dogs to see him pitch six or seven times. But apparently the Red Sox had their reservations.

It had been that way a few years before for another one of Rolfe's Legion protégés—pitcher Kenny Reynolds. He made it all the way to the San Diego Padres, where he still was in the 1975 season. Rolfe felt that both Reynolds and Fidrych would have been lured by Red Sox contracts, but none were offered.

Fidrych's high school career was not as brilliant as his Legion performances. As a freshman playing for the jayvee team, he did beat the varsity.

In his best year, as a junior in 1973, he was only 4–2 for Algonquin High. But his coach, Jack Wallace, remembered him having an arm problem that kept him out of the important last month of the season. His losses came on 4–3 and 2–1 scores. In one of those two defeats, his third baseman made three errors in one inning.

Fidrych, according to Wallace, was somewhat displeased that some teammates weren't working as hard as he was.

Wallace enjoyed coaching Mark, though they did have one run-in when he was a junior and wanted to pitch in an intrasquad scrimmage wearing a T-shirt. Wallace didn't think that was a good idea with the temperature at about 35 degrees.

The New York Yankees, the Cincinnati Reds, and the Minnesota Twins were frequent visitors to his games, though Wallace felt that Fidrych's arm problem may have touted them off his prospect.

As a senior, Mark would be nineteen, and not eligible to pitch for Algonquin High, which was under the auspices of the Massachusetts High School Athletic Association.

So his father enrolled him in Worcester Academy, a prep school in the nearby town where he taught.

Worcester played its games against other prep schools and college freshman teams.

But Fidrych recalls having a losing season his senior year. He could have gone to college—he had offers from assorted schools, including Old Dominion in Virginia and New Mexico Highlands—but he planned to stay around Northboro instead.

"I didn't expect to be drafted," he said. "Nobody even talked to me."

But that didn't mean he didn't have some big-league aspirations.

When he was pitching Legion ball, he used to tell his mother: "Someday I'm going to be in the majors."

Her reaction, in the way she liked to josh with him, would be to say: "Aw, dream on, kid."

She thought he would wind up as a Catholic priest or a mechanic.

Mark kept working at his pitching, throwing in the backyard between work and games.

His dedication paid off in June 1974 when the Detroit Tigers made him their tenth-round choice.

It was no big deal. More than two hundred players were taken before him.

The Tigers hadn't even been in evidence during the scouting process. But Joe Cusick, their New England scout, had been keeping notes on the tall right-hander and sending them to the front office in Detroit.

Cusick had Fidrych listed as the seventh best player in his area, a pretty good evaluation. The Fidrychs were somewhat surprised when Cusick finally made his appearance, though.

"How come you're here now?" Paul Fidrych asked him, concerned that the Tigers may not have put much importance in his son. "Where have you been?"

Cusick explained that he had been in the background, and did, indeed, know all about the boy. He sent in good reports—a young strong-arm kid who wasn't muscle-bound across the chest, a fastball pitcher, a worker, a player who loved the game. The so-called flaky stuff never appeared on the scouting report.

When Paul Fidrych got the word from the Tigers, he dashed down to the gas station where Mark was working.

"You don't have to work here anymore," the father said. "You got another job. The Tigers want you."

But even Paul Fidrych could never imagine how fast the Tigers wanted him.

In less than two years time, Mark Fidrych's picture would be on the front page of the Northboro

Evening-Gazette. Above the picture would be an eight-column headline, proclaiming:

NORTHBORO GOES NATIONAL WITH MARKIE FIDRYCH

GAME PLAYED MAY 25

DETROIT	ab	r	h	bi
LeFlore cf	4	0	1	0
AJohnson lf	4	0	1	0
Staub rf	4	0	1	0
Horton dh	4	0	0	0
JThompson 1b	4	0	1	0
ARodriguez 3b	4	0	1	0
Veryzer ss	4	0	0	0
Kimm c	3	0	2	0
Meyer ph	1	0	0	0
Manuel 2b	3	0	0	0
Fidrych p	0	0	0	0
Total	35	0	7	0

BOSTON	ab	r	h	bi
RiMiller lf	4	0	0	0
Doyle 2b	4	0	1	0
Lynn cf	4	0	1	0
Fisk c	3	1	0	0
Ystrmski 1b	4	1	1	2
Rice dh	3	0	1	0
DEvans rf	3	0	1	0
Petrocelli 3b	2	0	0	0
Burleson ss	3	0	1	0
Tiant p	0	0	0	0
Total	30	2	6	2

```
DETROIT ............................................. 000 000 000—0
BOSTON  ............................................. 000 200 000—2
```

E—Fisk, Burleson, Manuel, Petrocelli. LOB—Detroit 8, Boston 6. 2B—LeFlore, D.Evans. HR—Yastrzemski (8). SB—A. Johnson.

	IP	H	R	ER	BB	SO
Fidrych (L, 1—1)	8	6	2	2	2	1
Tiant (W, 6—2)	9	7	0	0	0	8

T—1:57. A—21,033.

Monday, May 31
VS. MILWAUKEE

The batter was Henry Aaron, The Hammer, the man who broke Babe Ruth's legendary lifetime home-run record before Mark Fidrych had graduated from high school.

For once, as Mark stood on the mound, hunched over from the waist, his feet together, his hands joined in readiness in front of him, The Bird knew exactly who he was up against.

It was the first inning of Fidrych's third start. He had been beaten by Boston last time out, and now it was up to him to prove that his initial victory over the Cleveland Indians hadn't been a fluke.

Milwaukee's Darrell Porter stood on first base, put there by an error by Gary Sutherland. And Hank Aaron stood waiting, bat in hand, at home plate. Hank Aaron, who'd hit his first big-league home run before Fidrych was born.

"You wonder what a guy like that is going to do," admitted Fidrych, who usually doesn't even know the batter's name. "But you can't get scared. If you're scared of a guy, nine times out of ten he'll beat you.

"It's like a war. You've got to have a feeling in you, but you've got to keep it out. So you pitch to Aaron like you'd pitch to anyone else. You go at him."

Fidrych went at Aaron, all right. He struck him out.

"The big thing wasn't that I struck out Henry Aaron," The Bird insisted afterward. "It was the third out of the inning, with a man on base, so the big thing was getting out of the inning. It was a good time for a strikeout."

Taking their cue from the curly-haired pitcher on the mound, the Tigers came through in the clutch that evening, too. It seemed as if The Bird had inspired them.

Twice the Tigers appeared doomed—and twice they battled back, so that all Fidrych's efforts and antics would not be in vain. Eventually, they edged the Milwaukee Brewers, 5–4, on Tom Veryzer's two-out single in the bottom of the eleventh inning.

It was a welcome win—and a scene that was to be repeated several times in the weeks ahead, as Fidrych's magic began to work wonders.

It took his teammates eleven innings to get him

the runs he needed to win his next game, too. In fact, in each of his next three starts, Fidrych would succeed by the slimmest of margins, one run.

The Tigers were quickly coming to believe in The Bird. You could actually sense the sudden confidence his teammates possessed each time Mark sprinted out to the mound.

The standing ovations from the audience and unprecedented curtain calls after each game were still in the future, but the partisan crowd of 17,894 at Tiger Stadium on Memorial Day repeatedly let Fidrych know they appreciated his performance as he battled the Brewers.

"It gave my body a rush," The Bird said later, when he was asked if he had heard all the cheering. "Any player gets a rush when he hears that from the stands. My mind's not that blank."

As Fidrych mowed down opponent after opponent, conquering every club he encountered, one by one, they each kicked themselves because they each knew The Bird could easily have belonged to them.

Baltimore could have drafted Fidrych. Then The Bird would have been an Oriole.

Boston could have picked him. And the hometown boy from up the road in Northboro would have packed Fenway Park.

New York had ample opportunity to select Fidrych, too. And you can imagine what would have happened if the New York press had gotten their hands on The Bird. Why, he might already be in the Hall of Fame.

The Tigers didn't pick Fidrych until the tenth round of the free-agent draft in June 1974—after all twenty-four major-league clubs had passed him over and drafted somebody else at least nine times.

The best brains in the baseball business rated two hundred and thirty-one young amateur prospects ahead of Fidrych that year.

The Bird was the two hundred and thirty-second player picked!

But, of the two hundred and thirty-one players picked ahead of him, only five—Butch Wynegar, Pete Vukovich, Jack Kusick, Mike Miley, and Tom Boggs—made it to the major leagues as quick as, or quicker than, Fidrych.

And only Butch Wynegar, the Minnesota Twins' highly regarded rookie catcher, attracted a comparable amount of attention and acclaim.

Incredibly, the Tigers almost overlooked Fidrych, too.

If it hadn't been for Joe Cusick, The Bird might be pumping gas today.

Cusick, who was then the Tigers' scout in the New England area, happened to see Fidrych throw one pitch one afternoon and called Detroit to say he had discovered a kid he considered worth drafting.

"It was three days before we were going to New York for the draft," recalled Bill Lajoie, whose job it is to keep the Tiger farm system stocked with fresh talent. "We had our list of the players we were interested in all made out.

"I remember when Joe called and gave me Fidrych's name, I wrote it down at the bottom of the sheet, then drew an arrow up to where Joe thought we should draft him. He wanted us to take him somewhere between the seventh and tenth rounds.

"I don't like to make last-minute changes like that," continued Lajoie. "But Joe said this was a kid he really wanted. He rated him the third or fourth best prospect of all the kids he had seen. But he said Mark wasn't very well known so we didn't have to be concerned about some other club grabbing him ahead of us."

The Tigers drafted Fidrych on the tenth round and offered him a bonus of about $10,000—although more than half of that sum was contingent upon his moving up through the minor leagues and eventually making it to the majors.

In fact, Fidrych advanced through the Tiger farm system so fast he collected the final $7,500 of that bonus shortly after the Milwaukee game, when he finished his first sixty days in the major leagues.

"I was a janitor in a gas station, working for two dollars an hour when the Tigers picked me," recalled Fidrych. "I couldn't believe it. I would have signed for free.

"Joe Cusick signed me after seeing me throw one pitch. I was playing left field in high school one day. The coach called me in to throw to one batter. I got him out on one pitch. I had no idea anyone was interested in me.

"I never really thought about playing pro baseball until I got drafted," continued Fidrych. "But when it happened, I said, 'Wow! They're giving you a shot. Grab it.'

"When I was a kid I never really thought about playing baseball. I was thinking about other things. Like I always wanted to own a '57 Chevy and hop it up. I was always looking forward to that.

"Now I can get it, but that scene's out, you know what I mean? I've put all those other things aside. But I can still go back to them if I want to."

After he signed, the Tigers sent Fidrych to Bristol, Virginia, in the Appalachian Rookie League, which is as low as you can go in their farm system. Because his class at Worcester Academy graduated late, Fidrych was one of the last players to report to Bristol that summer—but it didn't take him long to make an impression.

He had no sooner set foot on the field, on his first day in professional baseball, when he startled everyone with the high, shrieking squawk that would soon become his trademark.

"Gaawk! Gaawk!" exclaimed Fidrych as he galloped around the field.

"A bird—you're a bird," declared Bristol Coach Jeff Hogan.

And the nickname stuck.

There were fifteen pitchers at Bristol that summer, but Fidrych nevertheless distinguished himself by compiling an unblemished 3–0 record, an impressive 2.38 earned-run average, and a total of 40 strikeouts in 34 innings of relief.

"He talked like the devil, to the ball and to everyone else," recalled Joe Lewis, who managed the Bristol team. "He was just intense. And he really worked hard. He really pitched for me.

"He was so reliable I started using him all the time. One bit of trouble and I'd send him in and he'd get them out. I was worried about overworking him, that's how much I found myself relying on him.

"One time I had to send him to the showers, even though he wasn't pitching," continued Lewis. "Things weren't going so well one night and I was looking around the dugout, and there he was. I knew that if I didn't send him out of sight, I'd probably put him in the game again when he really should rest.

"So about halfway through the game I said, 'Bird, get a shower.' He didn't know what was going on. But I figured if he was in street clothes, I couldn't use him."

"That first year was really something," remembered Fidrych with a smile. "They wouldn't let you bring your car with you and you ended up hitchhiking home late at night after a ballgame, and all kinds of weird people would try to pick you up.

"You were always hungry, too. You could eat all your meal money at one meal. Then you had nothing left for the rest of the day."

It was at Bristol that the Tigers first began to

suspect that Fidrych might be something special.

"There was another pitcher on that team we had drafted in the eleventh round, right after Mark," recalled Bill Lajoie. "His name was Steve Gambey, and you couldn't tell the two of them apart.

"They looked alike, and they threw alike. They were both good prospects. The scouting reports on the two of them were very similar. You couldn't tell which one was going to be the better pitcher."

One year later, while Fidrych was wowing them in the big leagues, Gambey was home, helping his father on their farm.

"That's the way it happens—one falls by the wayside and one makes it big," Lajoie continued. "It has to do with the makeup of a player—not necessarily just his ability.

"Physically, Fidrych and Gambey were twins. They had the same arm action, the same windup, the same everything. At the end of that first year, Gambey was rated as a prospect with average major-league ability across the board and good aptitude. We gave Fidrych a plus on his fastball, but he didn't have as good a curveball as Gambey did.

"We had five pitchers on that team who we considered major-league prospects," said Lajoie. "Mark was one of them but he didn't look that much more outstanding than any of the others."

In 1975, Fidrych started the season at Lakeland, in the Class A Florida State League. It was the next logical step after Bristol.

And although he lost nine games while winning only five, Fidrych continued to impress people with his potential. And his eccentricity.

"When we first got him he'd come into the dugout after the first inning and go right over to the john and throw up," recalled Stubby Overmire, who managed The Bird at Lakeland for the first three months of 1975. "I'd ask him if he was all right and he'd say, 'Sure. I always do that.'"

Even then, Fidrych was forever talking to himself, and to the baseball.

"He was liable to say any damn thing that came into his mind," said Overmire. "But his concentration was incredible. When he was on the mound, he didn't know anyone else was in the park.

"He was real enthusiastic. And the fans liked him because he hustled. He was on and off the mound in a hurry. He pitched real fast games.

"All I ever saw him wear were cut-offs and a ragged shirt," continued Overmire. "Blue jeans and a T-shirt. He wasn't what you'd call Beau Brummell. And he walked like a plow jockey. He always looked like he had one foot in a furrow."

In spite of his eccentricities, and his unsatisfactory record, the Tigers still regarded The Bird as a top pitching prospect.

"I figured he had a good arm and I figured he'd play in the major leagues someday," said Overmire. "But not this quick. I'm not Einstein."

Though he consistently pitched well, Mark couldn't seem to win at Lakeland. He kept losing close games, usually by one or two runs. So Hoot

Evers, the former Tiger outfielder who now runs
the club's farm system, called The Bird aside one
day and told him he was being promoted.

"You're too good a pitcher to be five and nine,"
Evers told him. "I'm going to move you up to
Montgomery."

Fidrych was surprised. After all, Montgomery
was a step up in the minor leagues, in the Class
AA Southern League. A step closer to the big
leagues that still seemed so very far away.

"I was down at Lakeland," admitted Fidrych.
"Everyone was. I think they sent me to Montgomery to improve my morale."

But Fidrych spent only fifteen days at Montgomery, appearing in seven games and posting a
2–0 record, again pitching in relief.

Then up in Detroit, the Tigers' relief ace, John
Hiller, hurt his arm, Gene Pentz was hurriedly
called up from the Tigers top farm club at Evansville to replace him, and Fidrych was promoted to
Evansville to replace Pentz.

"We were in Orlando [Florida] when our trainer, Kenny Houston, told me I was going to Evansville the next morning," Fidrych recalled. "Wow!
I was shocked, but I was so happy. I got the idea
Evansville wanted me right away so I joined the
club in Wichita without going back to Montgomery to get my clothes.

"We were on a fifteen-day trip when I got the
news, so I had some extra clothes. But the first day
I got to Wichita I went out and bought some new

clothes with my meal money. You get more meal in Triple A, you know."

It was at Evansville that the Tiger organization really began to take notice of Fidrych. He was four and one, with a 1.59 earned-run average, pitching against the best minor leaguers in the country.

And he also enhanced his reputation for being a bit of a flake.

For instance, before Fidrych went out to pitch against Omaha in the game that would clinch the divisional title for Evansville in the American Association, he approached Manager Fred Hatfield and told him to order a case of champagne.

"Tonight," promised The Bird, "we celebrate."

"Tonight," promised Hatfield, "I'll break every bottle over your head if we don't win."

The Bird won, all right, 2–1. And the first thing he did when the game was over was gallop to home plate, where he gave his catcher, Gene Lamont, a big kiss. Then he wheeled and raced out into center field, where Art James had caught the ball for the last out. He gave him a hug and a kiss, too.

Later, in the Junior World Series, which Evansville eventually won, when Fidrych lost to Tidewater, 1–0, he went around the locker room and thanked each of his teammates for keeping the game so close. And he meant it.

By the end of the summer, word of his antics— and his ability—had reached Detroit, where the Tigers were in the process of finishing dead last in the American League East for the second year in a row, this time with the worst record in all of big-league baseball.

It was obvious the Tigers needed all the help they could get. But, as yet, they had no idea how much help this skinny young man was going to be.

Although the Tigers didn't put Fidrych on the major-league roster and bring him to Detroit to spend September acquainting himself with big leagues, as they did with some of their other top prospects, The Bird was in the backs of their minds when they began thinking ahead to 1976.

"If we had been in a pennant race, we might have brought him up," said Ralph Houk. "But that would have meant we would have had to put him on the roster and protect him in the draft, and there was no need for us to do that."

The Tigers weren't about to let The Bird go.

When they sat down with the Houston Astros after the the disastrous 1975 season and began to put together the deal that eventually brought catcher Milt May and pitchers Dave Roberts and Jim Crawford to Detroit, the Astros immediately asked for Fidrych.

But the Tigers refused to give him up, and Houston finally settled for two other top pitching prospects, Mark Lemongello and Gene Pentz, in addition to outfielder Leon Roberts and reserve catcher Terry Humphrey.

"I'll be honest with you. Most of us had Fidrych No. 1 on our lists," said Hoot Evers. "We had him zeroed in. If we had had to make a choice and rate somebody on top of the others, he would have been the one.

"A lot of other clubs were interested in him. He got a lot of good exposure pitching in the Junior World Series. People knew he could pitch.

"But I never had any idea he could pitch like this," Evers admitted. "I'd figured we'd have to send him to Evansville for another year to see if he was for real.

"But some guys just rise to the occasion. Fidrych has just got *that* something.

"He's no put-on," continued Evers. "He's the genuine article. Oh, he might carry on a little now because he sees how the fans have taken to him. But, really, what you see is what the boy actually is. He's genuine—and he's a nice kid.

"He's no genius, but he may be smarter than most of us. You've got to hand it to him. He backs up what he says.

"He says he doesn't need a lot of money to live, but he's interested in money, and he's willing to work hard to get it. And if he keeps this up, he'll get plenty."

During the Tigers' minor-league training camp, in the spring of 1975, Fidrych approached Evers and asked if he could hold a car wash on the abandoned airfield that now serves as the camp parking lot.

"He charged a buck and a half and got some of the other players to help him," recalled Evers.

"Nobody had ever done anything like that before."

But then The Bird did a lot of things no one had ever done before.

"One night I was driving back to camp," recalled Evers, "and I saw this strange figure hitchhiking on the road. He had no shirt on, just cut-off jeans, and tennis shoes that had to be at least ten years old. And his body was baked sun red. It was Mark.

"He had been on the beach all afternoon and was trying to get back to camp before curfew. Naturally, I picked him up.

"'Of all the luck,' he said when he got into the car. 'All the cars that go by and I gotta get picked up by my boss.'

"'What are you worrying about?' I said. 'You're not late for curfew yet. But you better be able to pitch tomorrow.' And he was.

"He didn't draw the crowds in the minors," said Evers. "They pooh-poohed what he did. Running in and out of the dugout isn't unusual down there.

"But he ran faster than anyone else. The other players didn't know just how to take him. At first, they thought he was trying to show them up. They had never seen anybody like this kid, always congratulating them for a good play.

"He must carry a sugar tank inside him. But drugs? Not Mark. I asked him once if he had ever smoked pot and he said, 'I don't have any need for it.'"

GAME PLAYED MAY 31

MILWAUKEE	ab	r	h	bi	DETROIT	ab	r	h	bi
Yount ss	6	1	2	1	LeFlore cf	4	1	2	1
Money 3b	6	1	1	3	Veryzer ss	5	0	2	2
Porter c	5	0	0	0	Staub rf	4	0	3	1
Aaron dh	4	0	1	0	Horton dh	5	0	2	0
Lezcano pr	0	0	0	0	AJohnson lf	5	0	1	0
GScott 1b	3	0	1	0	JThompson 1b	5	0	0	0
Sharp rf	3	0	2	0	ARodriguez 3b	3	0	0	0
CMoore lf	2	0	0	0	Meyer ph	1	0	0	0
Hansen ph	1	0	0	0	Scrivener 3b	1	1	1	0
Rosario lf	2	1	1	0	Kimm c	3	0	1	0
GThomas cf	4	0	0	0	Oglivie ph	1	1	1	0
PGarcia 2b	5	1	3	0	Wocknfus c	1	0	0	0
Slaton p	0	0	0	0	Sutherland 2b	3	0	1	0
Murphy p	0	0	0	0	MStanley ph	1	1	1	1
Augustine p	0	0	0	0	Manuel 2b	1	1	1	0
Sprague p	0	0	0	0	Fidrych p	0	0	0	0
Total	41	4	11	4	Total	43	5	16	5

Two out when winning run scored

MILWAUKEE .... 000 000 300 01—4
DETROIT .... 000 001 002 02—5

E—Sutherland, P.Garcia, Veryzer, Sharp. DP—Milwaukee 3, Detroit 3. LOB—Milwaukee 10, Detroit 10. 2B—P.Garcia, Kimm, Oglivie. 3B—LeFlore, 2. HR—Money (5). SB—Manuel. S—Sharp. SF—Veryzer, LeFlore.

	IP	H	R	ER	BB	SO
Slaton	7	9	1	1	1	5
E. Rodriguez	1⅓	2	2	2	1	0
Murphy	⅓	0	0	0	0	0
Augustine	⅓	1	0	0	0	0
Sprague (L, 0—2)	1⅔	4	2	1	0	0
Fidrych (W, 2—1)	11	11	4	4	4	8

HBP—by Fidrych (Sharp). WP—Slaton, Fidrych. T—3:04. A—17,894.

Saturday, June 5
AT TEXAS

Every seat in Arlington Stadium was occupied when Mark Fidrych sprinted out of the dugout to take on the Texas Rangers on June 5.

But, it was safe to say, not one of the 36,825 jammed into the ballpark had come to see The Bird.

Because it was on this hot, humid evening that Bert Blyleven, the high-priced pitcher who was supposed to bring the Rangers the pennant, would make his debut in a Texas uniform.

Before long, Fidrych would attract crowds like that himself, everywhere he pitched. But for the moment, the overwhelming majority of the fans had never heard of The Bird.

That made it even. Because The Bird had never heard of Bert Blyleven, either.

Things would be quite different when the Tigers

would return to Texas one month later. By then Fidrych would be a full-fledged national celebrity, and the switchboard at Arlington Stadium would be bombarded with telephone calls demanding to know when The Bird was going to pitch.

Even though Fidrych didn't pitch in that second series, much to the Rangers' financial regret, he was besieged by autograph seekers every time he stuck his head out of the Tigers' dugout.

The Bird tried to oblige them all. He stood for twenty to thirty minutes at a time, each day, doing nothing but signing his name for people who, a month earlier, weren't even aware that Mark Fidrych existed.

Still some of the fans weren't satisfied.

One young man reached over the railing while The Bird was busy scrawling his name on still another scrap of paper and snatched his Tiger cap right off his head.

While the teenager dashed up through the nearly empty stands to safety, Fidrych stood screaming on the field, threatening to run after the thief. That was the thanks he got for trying to be a nice guy and give autographs.

Moments later, another in the endless stream of photographers tapped Fidrych on the shoulder and asked him to pose for a picture. With his cap on, of course.

Turning to two teammates sitting in the dugout, The Bird asked if he could borrow one of their caps. Both smiled and said no, and sat back to enjoy The Bird's dilemma.

Thoroughly frustrated by now, Fidrych approached Coach Joe Schultz, borrowed his cap—which, of course, didn't fit—stood still long enough for the photographer to snap a couple of quick pictures, then galloped off to the safety of the outfield.

But on June 5, all that hysteria was still a month away.

This time, Fidrych warmed up unnoticed down the left-field line. Then, while the eyes of Texas were all on Blyleven, The Bird stole the show, outdueling the Texas ace, 3–2, in eleven muggy innings.

"Far out," exclaimed Fidrych, as he slumped on the stool in front of his locker just long enough to wipe the beads of sweat off his brow. "What else can I say? This is a rush.

"It was a little weird to look around and see that many people just for a game," he admitted, never dreaming of what lay ahead. "But I liked the big crowd. It was a defensive crowd."

Asked what he meant by a "defensive crowd," Fidrych jumped to his feet.

"Look, man, they were booing me, weren't they," he explained. "They don't boo you on the road when you're losing. And I knew they weren't booing Blyleven. So it had to be me. It psyched me up.

"I didn't know who Blyleven was," admitted Fidrych. "Let's put it this way: It was like me pitching against any other guy. He [Blyeven] is not the guy beating me. It's their batters who are beating me."

In the seventh inning, Fidrych suffered a spike wound on his right foot when he sprinted over to cover first base on a double play attempt by the Tigers.

As he lay on the ground, surrounded by Bill Behm, the Tigers' team trainer, and several sympathetic teammates, it looked for a moment like The Bird might have to leave the game.

"I don't see any bones sticking out," cackled Ralph Houk, as he leaned over his rookie pitcher and tried to cheer him up.

"That's right," yelped Fidrych, leaping to his feet. "There's no bones showing. Let's go."

The Bird strutted back to the mound and shut the Rangers out the rest of the night, until his teammates finally rallied and got him the runs he required in the eleventh inning.

After the game, it took three stitches to sew up the slice in Fidrych's foot.

But the only thing that really hurt was the fact that the doctor said there was nothing he could do about the big gash Texas' Juan Beniquez had made in one of The Bird's new shoes.

Until he made the major-league team in the spring of 1976, Fidrych never knew what it was like to have a locker full of baseball shoes—all of them given to him by the manufacturer, for free.

Although they never came right out and said so at the time, the Tigers—meaning Manager Ralph Houk and General Manager Jim Campbell—felt

Fidrych was going to make the team before spring training ever began.

It is commonly assumed that The Bird made the team with his strong showing in the spring exhibition games.

But that's simply not true.

As a matter of fact he didn't pitch particularly well at all in the spring.

As Houk put it: "He didn't pitch good, and he didn't pitch bad."

Fidrych only pitched three times in spring training, which was shortened by the hassle between the owners and the players' union, which resulted in a lockout by the owners.

Many assumed that because the training camps didn't open until the middle of March, young, promising but unproven pitchers like Fidrych wouldn't have much of a chance.

But Houk claimed he had already made up his mind about The Bird.

"We certainly intended to keep him, unless something happened like an injury, or he was just awful," stated Houk, who kept everyone, including Fidrych, in suspense right up until the final cuts were made, one week before the club broke camp and headed for Cleveland and the opening of the regular season.

"When I saw him pitch in the fall of seventy-five at Dunedin [The Tigers' entry in the prestigious Florida Instructional League] I knew he was going to be a major-league pitcher," Houk said.

"But there was no reason to put him on the major-league roster during the winter. We didn't have to protect him. He had options left. So why put him on the roster? If he had gotten hurt or something, then we would have wasted one of his options.

"There was no need to put him on the major-league roster in the spring, either. But we were counting on him to be one of our regular starters."

No one was more surprised than The Bird when, in the middle of a routine clubhouse meeting, he found out he had made the team.

"I started to stand up, and my knees were shaking so much I couldn't stand," recalled Fidrych, who had already resigned himself to spending the summer at Evansville.

"I'll tell you, man, that was the rush of my life. I'll never have another high like that. It's not every day a kid makes a major-league team. I'm one in a million. That's a rush."

The Bird borrowed a dime and called his parents in Massachusetts, collect, to give them the incredible news. Then he asked Vince Desmond, the Tigers' traveling secretary, if that meant he would now get major-league meal money, too, instead of having to stand in line to eat in the minor-league cafeteria.

The next day, Tiger General Manager Jim Campbell took The Bird shopping in downtown Lakeland.

After all, the Tigers don't travel in T-shirts and

blue jeans—and that was all Campbell had ever seen Fidrych wear.

His dress, in fact, was the talk of the Tigers' training camp.

Each day, Fidrych would show up at Marchant Stadium in Lakeland in his vintage blue jeans, his faded, loosely fitting blue shirt, which looked like the pajama tops somebody's great-grandfather had given to Goodwill, and his infamous sneakers with the torn soles and knotted laces.

Hoot Evers claimed you could smell The Bird's shoes any time you got within five feet of them. "If you ever had a bad head," said Evers, "all you had to do was walk by The Bird's locker. Those shoes would clear your head in a hurry."

One day Evers sarcastically asked Fidrych if he would will those shoes to him, when he died.

"I want to have them bronzed," explained Evers, with a straight face.

"I think he thought I was serious," recalled the Tigers' farm director. "He looked up and said, 'Sure, but I'm not quite through with them yet.'"

Anyway, when Fidrych and Campbell arrived at the clothing store, the day after The Bird made the team, the Tiger executive told the young pitcher to pick out a couple of leisure suits for himself.

Fidrych first inspected a few of the cheaper models, and even then appeared in awe of the price tags.

Campbell noticed and said, "Don't worry. Pick

out what you like. These are on the Detroit ball-club."

Hearing that, Fidrych sprinted to the high-priced rack, pausing to grab a few shirts along the way.

When he reported to training camp with his curly blond hair hanging down over his shoulders, he was immediately ordered to get a haircut.

So he turned in a bill for $5 to the front office on an expense voucher.

It was rejected, of course, but people remembered.

Fidrych faced the St. Louis Cardinals, Boston Red Sox, and Cincinnati Reds in the spring, working a fraction more than nine innings, losing his only decision and accumulating an unimpressive 4.66 earned-run average.

But The Bird was the talk of spring training—not only in the Tiger camp but in the camps of the Cardinals, Red Sox, and Reds as well.

The Cardinals were all over Fidrych from their dugout when he went into his now-familiar routine against them, aiming the ball and talking to himself.

Three scoreless innings later, the St. Louis dugout was silent. Mark Fidrych's first exhibition game had been a success.

While Ralph Houk played down the importance of that performance in his conversations with the press, preferring to point out that it had merely been a non-roster rookie's first game, the Tiger manager was nonetheless pleased.

Fidrych's next spring start came against the Red Sox, and Marchant Stadium was filled that evening. In addition, the game was being televised back to Boston, and to Northboro, where Mark knew his family and friends would be watching.

The Bird was warming up in the bullpen, just beyond the first base bleachers, when he suddenly realized he had forgotten to insert his protective cup into his athletic supporter.

So, without a word to anyone, he sprinted off the mound and into the clubhouse. Moments later he came racing back, cup in hand. Then, standing there on the bullpen mound, in full view of anyone who happened to be looking, he lowered his trousers and put the protective cup in place.

Then he continued to warm up for the game.

Even warming up in the bullpen, Fidrych was oblivious to everyone and everything around him.

Boston's Bernie Carbo began the game with a base hit. Fidrych immediately went into a monologue on the mound and gestured almost frantically with his hands. The next three Boston batters went out one-two-three. And The Bird almost flew into the Tiger dugout.

The first batter up in the Red Sox second inning was twelve-time All-Star Carl Yastrzemski. But Fidrych scarcely noticed.

"Hey, I heard when they announced some guy like Yaz, but I forgot it quick," he said.

Finally, in the third inning, the Red Sox broke Fidrych's skein of five consecutive scoreless innings, eventually building up a 10–0 lead against

The Bird and his replacement, Tiger reliever Dave Lemanczyk.

His teammates didn't help matters any when they suddenly forgot how to hang on to the ball, but Fidrych refused to blame anyone but himself.

"Hey, I'll clue you, these guys behind me are the best I've ever had behind me," he said. "You know, I never played college ball, but I can sure tell you there's a lot of difference between these guys and high school fielding.

"I used to be a poor sportsman," continued Fidrych. "When I was a kid, like in Little League, if a teammate made an error I'd get all over him. It was wrong when I did that. Now when I look back on it, I realize it was wrong. I say to myself, 'Wow, I never should have done that.'

"Maybe it was because I was so keyed up all the time, and the other guys didn't think so much about that game. I don't know why I did it. But I was a bad guy."

Fidrych's final exhibition outing came against the World Champion Cincinnati Reds, the best team in all of baseball the summer before. Like the Cardinals and the Red Sox, the Reds were mildly amused as they watched the gangling young man do his thing on the mound.

But that was all they got from Fidrych—a few chuckles—as The Bird held them hitless for three innings.

While Fidrych was making such an impression on everyone else, though, he remained refreshingly unaware of where he was or what was going on around him.

He was sitting on the porch outside the Tigers' clubhouse with minor-league pitcher Dave Rozema before an exhibition game against the New York Yankees when Bob Sullivan, a former player and part-time Tiger scout, who was standing nearby, decided to do the kids a favor and introduce them to an old friend who happened to be passing by.

Sullivan made the introductions, and everyone said hello and shook hands, and the man in the Yankee uniform wished both young pitchers luck, then walked away.

When he left, Fidrych turned to Rozema and inquired, "Who was that guy anyway?"

It was Billy Martin, probably the best-known manager in the American League.

GAME PLAYED JUNE 5

DETROIT	ab	r	h	bi	TEXAS	ab	r	h	bi
Scrivener 2b	4	2	1	0	Clines lf	5	1	1	0
Meyer lf	5	0	2	0	Pryor 2b	4	0	0	0
Staub rf	4	0	2	1	Hargrove 1b	5	0	0	1
Horton dh	5	0	1	0	Harrah ss	5	0	2	1
Oglivie cf	5	1	1	0	Buroghs rf	4	0	1	0
JThompson 1b	4	0	0	0	Howell 3b	4	0	1	0
ARodrigez 3b	5	0	2	0	Grieve dh	4	0	1	0
Kimm c	5	0	1	1	Beniquez cf	4	0	0	0
Sutherland 2b	2	0	0	0	Sundberg c	4	1	2	0
AJohnson ph	1	0	0	0	Blyleven p	0	0	0	0
Manuel ph	0	0	0	0					
LeFlore ph	1	0	0	0					
MStanley ss	1	0	0	0					
Fidrych p	0	0	0	0					
Total	42	3	10	2	Total	39	2	7	2

DETROIT .... 000 001 010 01—3
TEXAS .... 002 000 000 00—2

E—Harrah, Howell, Scrivener. DP—Texas 3. LOB—Detroit 9, Texas 6. 2B—Harrah, Pryor. SB—Oglivie. S—Pryor.

	IP	H	R	ER	BB	SO
Fidrych (W, 3—1)	11	7	2	2	1	8
Blyleven (L, 4—6)	11	10	3	2	3	10

T—2:42. A—32,678.

Friday, June 11
VS. CALIFORNIA

Pat Dobson ... Luis Tiant ... Jim Slaton ... Bert Blyleven ...

Now, Nolan Ryan.

No one could accuse the opposition of making life easy for Mark Fidrych. In his short major-league career, he had already faced some of the finest pitchers in the American League.

Except for Tiant, he had beaten them all. But it was pretty clear by now he was getting some help from his friends—his Tiger teammates.

In his victory over strikeout king Nolan Ryan, The Bird gave up a run in the first inning to the California Angels as the result of a throwing error by second-baseman Pedro Garcia.

But the Tigers got two back in the third and another in the fourth before the Angels tied it again, 3–3, in the sixth.

In between, there were a couple of thundershowers that delayed the game for a total of fifty-five minutes. The veteran, Ryan, couldn't cope with the interruptions and was pulled. The Bird pitched on.

As the game came down to the ninth inning, the 36,377 fans at Tiger Stadium were still hanging on.

The Angels threatened to score in the top of the ninth when Rusty Torres was thrown out at the plate by Garcia, and in the bottom of the inning Alex Johnson knocked Ron LeFlore home with the winning run on an exciting infield hit.

That gave The Bird three straight late-inning victories.

After the game, a reporter asked The Bird if, because of the way the team was coming through and the way everything right was happening to him, he felt destined to win games.

"What does destined mean?" he asked.

Whether or not he was destined for victory, Fidrych's teammates were doing their best to see that he got into the victory column. The Bird was the first to acknowledge that fact.

"Hey, these guys are making me," he'd say. "You know that. You know I couldn't do this without them. I can't believe what these guys are doing for me.

"These guys are making me—I'm not making them. If I was making myself, I'd be striking everybody out. If they don't play well behind me, I'm not even here."

The reporters had heard that before, and they would have to hear it again from The Bird before they could get to their routine questions when they talked to him.

Lots of players say the same thing. Lots of them mean it. But only The Bird insists that they get their due share, that they go out with him to share his successes, that they get properly thanked with handshakes and pats on the back after a good play or after a good game.

Only The Bird races to the dugout—other pitchers walk—so he can be there to greet his teammates and thank them for what they have done.

In games when he wasn't pitching, Manager Ralph Houk exiled him to the far end of the dugout, where he could yell all he wanted without breaking someone's eardrum.

But it was a fact that the team did play better for him.

"The players in the field are alert when the kid pitches because he throws strikes," said Houk. "They know they have to be on their toes every time he throws. He's also a strong finisher. They know they can win if they hang in there with him."

Fidrych had no problem being accepted by his Tiger teammates long before he starred for them. Going back to spring training, one of the first players to befriend him was Willie Horton, a veteran slugger and long-time favorite of the Detroit fans.

"Bird is one of the old-timers," said Horton. "You can tell about people. I sit back and observe.

"Now I look around and see everyone grabbing

him. But he knows what's going on. He's got a good head. He acts like he don't, but he's got a good mind.

"He knows who's with him and who's against him. It's easy for people to give advice now when he's good. But when you need it is when nobody is with you. Then you need somebody to make you feel at home."

In Florida, before Fidrych made his mark, Horton was already making The Bird feel like one of the gang.

Each spring, Horton, who has thirteen big-league seasons behind him, hosts cookouts for his teammates in the parking lot outside of the Holiday Inn where the Tigers stay in Lakeland. He fashioned a huge grill from a metal barrel. The sizzling steaks can be smelled two buildings away.

Fidrych was sequestered along with the rest of the minor leaguers in a dormitory on the abandoned air base that serves as the Tigers' training camp. Only those on the major-league roster stayed at the Holiday Inn.

But Horton was quick to invite the raw rookie to one of his first outings in the parking lot. Horton drove out to the dormitory, in what is called Tigertown, to pick up The Bird.

"I could tell he was everyday people," said Horton. "He wasn't trying to prove nothing to nobody. He was just being himself.

"I like the way he handles himself. I think he appreciates where he is. It's no accident he got here. Most young guys don't think like that. Bird's got a lot of ability, and he uses it."

It was a strange matchup—Horton, thirty-two, a veteran, short, black, a Detroit native, and Fidrych, twenty-one, a rookie, tall, white, a native of far-away Massachusetts.

But the friendship continued right into the regular season.

When the clubhouse attendant at Tiger Stadium, Jack Hand, decided he could no longer afford to provide soda pop for the players free of charge for the 1976 season, Horton and The Bird went into business for themselves. Horton brought a cooler from home and he and The Bird set up shop.

"The Boomer and The Bird . . . The B-and-B Pop Store," Horton proclaimed, laughing and shaking his head. "The guys don't have to pay for the pop," he explained. "If they want to give a donation, they can. Anything they want to give. But nobody has given one yet."

When Horton was injured and put on the disabled list in June, because of inflamed ligaments in his foot, Fidrych was put in charge of the pop store. When Horton returned a few weeks later to begin working out again, he found his partner in a frenzy.

"They robbed us blind," The Bird declared, trying to sound serious. "They wiped us out. They beat the *bleep* out of me and robbed us blind."

Horton wrapped one of his muscular arms around his trim teammate and gave him a consoling hug.

"I guess we're just going to have to restock the store," he said, laughing all the way.

Horton's attitude toward the player who was stealing all the headlines was typical of others on the club.

"There's not a thing contrived about him," said Rusty Staub, who has been a star himself with four clubs. "I've seen some guys do some stupid things for notoriety. But this is just Fidrych. He makes the whole team more enthusiastic.

"It's exhilarating to play when he pitches because there's an electricity that he brings out in everyone —the players and the fans. He brings out the exuberance and the youth in everybody.

"I've seen Tom Seaver [the New York Mets ace] mow 'em down, but I've never seen anyone electrify the fans like this."

One thing Fidrych does do to become part of the team is to follow tradition, not try to take it over. He's a good soldier that way.

In springtime, he was accepted by just about everyone, before and after he made the Tiger team.

As the team left spring training with Fidrych on the squad, he was rooming with veteran Joe Coleman, who had been a two-time twenty-game winner for the Tigers. When the team reached Cleveland for the opening series of the regular season, Fidrych wasn't sure of major-league protocol, or eating habits.

"What do we do for dinner?" he asked Coleman.

Coleman invited him out with three other players, including another new pitcher, Dave Roberts, who also had considerable major-league experience. Fidrych was the only neophyte among them.

Fidrych remembers the situation well. He wasn't in the best financial shape after leaving Florida, and there was no supplemental income to be had. He went along a bit guardedly. Then, as he recalled:

"The bill comes for dinner and Dave pays it. They say, 'It's okay.' Then we go out for some beers, and when I try to buy a round, they won't let me.

"I don't know what's going on, so I ask.

"They tell me this is the way it's done. When a rookie is on his first road trip, they take him out and show him around and treat him. They said someone did it for them and they wanted to do it for me."

A few weeks later, the Tigers brought up Jason Thompson, a very promising minor leaguer who had teamed with Fidrych for a while the year before. One of the first people to offer the newest rookie a helping hand was The Bird. Fidrych helped Thompson look for an apartment, and generally "tried to do for him what my teammates had done for me."

Thompson quickly added his name to The Bird's growing list of friends.

Fidrych's closest associate on the team undoubtedly was Tom Veryzer, his roommate on road trips and a neighbor in the apartment complex where he lives in Southgate.

The pitcher and shortstop Veryzer, twenty-three years old, make for an odd couple.

Unlike Fidrych, Veryzer rarely shows emotion at any level. Fidrych is shrill, loud, and a constant yakker. Veryzer says about ten words a year, and says them softly.

But Veryzer doesn't mind the matchup on road trips.

"It's good rooming with him," said Veryzer, who became the Tigers' regular shortstop in 1975. "I like to sleep late and he likes to sleep late. He sleeps a lot—at least ten hours a night. And he snores viciously. One night, he kept me awake until ten in the morning.

"Mostly, he'll relax and watch TV."

Veryzer said Fidrych wasn't as hyper as a roommate, but there were some exceptions.

"He'll be relaxing and then all of a sudden he'll jump off the bed and ask me if I want to fight him," Veryzer continued. "Or all of a sudden he'll yell something out. When he wants to say something, he just blurts it out of nowhere."

One thing Veryzer had to learn after Fidrych's instant fame was to keep the telephone off the receiver in their room, or let the desk accept the calls for screening. Otherwise, Veryzer said, a call every fifteen minutes would not be unusual. The calls are almost exclusively for Fidrych.

Veryzer still wouldn't trade him as a roommate.

"It's nice having somebody around whose hair is

longer than mine," the shortstop said. "It keeps the ballclub off my back."

Fidrych's mushrooming popularity in the first half of the season made him the focal point of the team's humor. When all the telephone calls began coming through the clubhouse phone, some team members stationed the phone on a little table next to his dressing cubicle.

The fan mail for Fidrych soon surpassed the total for the rest of the team as a whole.

The veteran players learned to move aside for autograph seekers and interviewers. John Hiller, the star relief pitcher, joked about moving his locker stall because of the crowd of reporters Fidrych began to draw after games he pitched. Hiller did move away after games, but not bitterly.

Hiller, like the other veterans—Bill Freehan, Mickey Stanley, Horton, others—got used to standing idle waiting for team planes and buses while the crowds congregated around Fidrych. At Detroit's Metropolitan Airport, where Fidrych is known best, businessmen with their briefcases, airline employees in coveralls with their lunch buckets, mothers with babies in their arms all vie for The Bird's attention, and his autograph.

Once a man approached Freehan, an eleven-time American League All-Star, and asked the catcher: "Which one of you is The Bird?"

Sometimes, The Bird is happy to have his teammates mistaken for him. While he enjoys the attention given him by female fans, it's good to have an out if he's not interested in a particular one.

When getting calls at the hotel or the clubhouse from girls asking for dates, Fidrych sometimes consents.

"At least I gotta check it out," he said. "If they're ugly, I'll just say, 'I'm Tom Veryzer—Mark Fidrych isn't here.'"

When a player gets as big as The Bird did, however, ballplayers inevitably get together to test his vulnerability.

Fidrych got it from all sides in one game when the Cleveland Indians planted a special ball, complete with an obscene inscription, on the mound when The Bird went out to pitch to them in the first inning.

"The first time he tries to talk to the baseball, it will have something to say to him," laughed Tom Buskey, the man who printed the message.

Fidrych picked up the ball, noticed the inscription, did a double-take, and flipped it to Coach Dick Tracewski, who flung it into the Indians' dugout.

How much that affected him is hard to say, but he did have one of his worst afternoons.

Fidrych was knocked out of that game, though the Tigers came back to win it. So his teammates decided to test their star under less happy circumstances.

The Bird had used an obscenity himself while being interviewed on national television after the game. It was a routine part of his language but apparently escaped the people who have the technical machinery to stop such flaws.

The following day, between games of a double-header, there was a telegram awaiting The Bird in the clubhouse. It read:

THIS IS TO INFORM YOU THAT YOU ARE HEREBY FINED $250 FOR USING PROFANITY ON THE NBC-TV GAME OF THE WEEK POST-GAME SHOW. SUCH REPREHENSIBLE CONDUCT CANNOT AND WILL NOT BE TOLERATED. ANY FURTHER SUCH ACTION COULD RESULT IN YOUR SUSPENSION. SIGNED: BOWIE K. KUHN. COMMISSIONER OF BASEBALL.

The telegram looked real and came in a Western Union envelope.

Fidrych leaped to his feet and went screaming into Manager Ralph Houk's office.

"Look at this! Look at this!" he exclaimed. "They can't do this to me, can they?"

"I'm afraid they can," said Houk, who had been advised in advance of the joke.

"Oh, this is awful. This is awful," Fidrych said. He returned to the clubhouse and began pacing back and forth the length of the room.

"Come on, you guys did this to me, didn't you?" he finally asked. "This is just a trick, right?"

But he wasn't convinced, and for ten minutes they weren't going to give him the satisfaction and security he badly wanted.

When he finally got the word that he had been duped, he took it in stride, smiled broadly, and then had to begin worrying about his wristwatch that a teammate had hidden.

"I've been decked out all day long," he said, shaking his curly head.

In the long run, even the seasoned big leaguers are going to remember Fidrych's feats and the reaction they touched off in 1976. But no one expressed it better than another rookie, The Bird's catcher, Bruce Kimm.

"He's the greatest thing that has happened to the game in a long time," said Kimm. "It's going to be talked about for a long, long time. And when I get old, I'll be able to say that I played with him, I caught him."

GAME PLAYED JUNE 11

CALIFORNIA	ab	r	h	bi	DETROIT	ab	r	h	bi
Bonds rf	4	1	2	0	LeFlore cf	5	1	1	0
Remy 2b	3	0	1	0	PGarcia 2b	4	1	1	0
RoJackson 3b	4	1	0	1	AJohnson lf	5	0	1	0
TDavis dh	4	0	1	1	Staub dh	2	1	1	0
Bochte lf	4	0	1	0	JThompson 1b	2	0	0	1
RTorres cf	0	0	0	0	Oglivie rf	4	0	1	1
Melton 1b	3	0	0	0	ARodriguez 3b	4	0	2	1
LStanton lf	4	0	2	0	Scrivener ss	3	0	0	0
MGuerro ss	4	0	1	0	Kimm c	3	1	1	0
Etchberrn c	3	1	1	0	Meyer ph	1	0	0	0
Ryan p	0	0	0	0	Fidrych p	0	0	0	0
Hartzell p	0	0	0	0					
Total	33	3	9	2	Total	33	4	8	3

Two out when winning run scored

```
CALIFORNIA ............................................. 100 002 000—3
DETROIT ................................................. 000 210 001—4
```

E—P.Garcia, Etchebarren, Scrivener, Hartzell, Remy. DP—Detroit 1. LOB—California 5, Detroit 9. 2B—L.Stanton, P. Garcia. SB—Bonds, Remy 2. S—Remy, Scrivener, Melton.

	IP	H	R	ER	BB	SO
Ryan	5	4	3	3	4	9
Hartzell (L, 0—2)	3⅔	4	1	0	1	3
Fidrych (W, 4—1)	9	9	3	1	0	4

WP—Ryan. T—2:28. A—36,377.

Wednesday, June 16
VS. KANSAS CITY

If there was any team that appeared capable of bringing The Bird down to earth, it had to be the Kansas City Royals. They were the best hitting team in the American League.

The night before he was scheduled to start against Kansas City, Fidrych was assigned the standard task of charting the pitches for that game, thus forcing him to watch the game in minute detail. The Royals, a team he had never seen play, gave him an eyeful.

He sat on his perch at the top step of the far end of the dugout and scribbled away. The Bird almost swallowed his bubble gum as the Royals blasted four Tiger pitchers for twenty-four hits and twenty-one runs.

It was hardly the type of game to bolster the confidence of an impressionable rookie, waiting in the wings for a chance at a real hitting team.

The Bird did get some advice from fellow pitcher Ray Bare, who told him the Royals' bats might be slow after all that hitting. Things don't work that way, though.

The next night, the new game featuring The Bird on the mound seemed like a mere continuation of the contest he charted.

The first three Royals to face him got on base, and in no time Kansas City grabbed a one-run lead.

Besides that, the Royals' batters were jumping in and out of the batter's box, believing that this would unnerve Fidrych.

Ralph Houk had to wonder if the miracle was coming to an end.

It wasn't. The Bird bore down. He gave up two more runs but made the Royals, boasting a team average of .295 going into the game, sweat for them. The Royals got only five hits, received only two walks from Fidrych, and finished the game with just two men left on base.

The Tigers got two home runs from Jason Thompson, then rallied for the winning runs in the 4–3 game in the bottom of the ninth.

The Bird said later he liked the close games, they kept his concentration sharp.

With the victory over such a good team as Kansas City, would-be critics and pessimists in general began to believe in Mark Fidrych.

Not only did he have a great attitude and a rare ability to stick to the game no matter what happened along the way, he was simply a good technical pitcher.

He consistently kept the ball low and he constantly threw strikes. That's not easy, at least not as easy as he made it appear.

For over a century, coaches and managers have been telling their pitchers to do the same thing. The ones who could became stars. That's what happened to Fidrych.

"He's got a very simplified idea of pitching," explained Hoot Evers, the Tigers' farm director, who has followed The Bird's professional career as closely as anyone. "He's pitching from strikes, not balls.

"You've got to realize a batter becomes a different kind of hitter when he's got one strike on him. The strike zone becomes larger and he can't take a chance on taking a pitch that's close to being a strike.

"And when you get two strikes on a batter, that strike zone suddenly becomes very large. The hitter is much more apt to swing at pitches that are a little off color because he doesn't want to take a chance on the umpire calling him out on strikes. And when he swings at a pitch like that, he's more apt to strike out. It's as simple as that."

Evers described Fidrych's fastball as "funny." It breaks late, according to Evers, and it moves right at the very end, jumping at the hitter. It goes past hitters low and fast. That gives them little time to react.

Fidrych has a wide variety of pitches. As a

youth, according to Ted Rolfe, who coached him in Legion ball, Mark had a good three-finger knuckleball, but the man who managed him for three years said the Tigers told him not to use it.

Rolfe has had a better vantage point from which to watch the technical side of Fidrych over the years, and after seeing him pitch a later game against the New York Yankees, he told about the chart he had kept. He noticed that The Bird threw only three high pitches until the last inning. Then his concentration was broken after a teammate got hurt. But The Bird came back with all good low pitches after he regained his concentration.

Fidrych's fastball has been timed at 93 miles per hour on three occasions by a special radarlike device ABC television uses during games. But at least one big-league scout, Frank Malzone of the Red Sox, has questioned such timing devices, though Malzone is quick to credit Fidrych's talents.

Over the years, The Bird's pitching style has remained the same. Bruce Kimm caught him in the minors before being assigned to catch Fidrych's every game in the majors. Kimm noticed no change at all when he began catching him for the Tigers in 1976.

"A person with all his antics," said Kimm, "you'd think he'd rush himself. But he's like a guy who's been around for fifteen years."

Kimm, and even veterans like Mickey Stanley, point to Fidrych as their stopper in case the team gets going badly, as it did for two years before Fidrych reached the majors.

"When we're playing bad, we know we can count on Mark," said Kimm. "He was that way with our team in Evansville, too."

Kimm at first couldn't understand why he got to catch Fidrych from the start in the majors. The Tigers started out the season with Milt May, a fine catcher they traded for, and Bill Freehan, the eleven-time All-Star. There also was John Wocken-fuss, who had big-league experience.

But Kimm apparently got the job of being Fidrych's exclusive catcher because of his experience with The Bird in the minors.

Bruce, a five-foot-eleven, 170-pounder, doesn't find his job all that hard.

"Mark is easy to catch," he said. "With him, when you want the ball in a certain area, it's there. The only thing I have to do is tell him to lay back and pop the ball and follow through.

"I don't even have to settle him down.

"He's got a lot of enthusiasm but he's got control of himself.

"I'll holler at him once in a while and tell him to lay back. And I tell him when he misses to miss low. I haven't had to say much to him, obviously.

"He's easy to work with because he'll listen to what I say and take what I say and evaluate it. If he has something to say to me, I'll listen and evaluate it. That's the way it should be between a pitcher and a catcher."

For the most part, Kimm is a quiet, likable player, who probably could not dominate a pitcher anyway. In Fidrych's case, that is certainly a plus.

"He gets everybody turned on," Kimm added. "He works hard, and it rubs off on the rest of us."

Kimm spoke of Fidrych's deep concentration:

"When he's out there on the mound, it's just him and the catcher. He doesn't even pay any attention to the hitter. A lot of the time, he doesn't even know who's up there. He's just going to pitch his game."

Fidrych thinks there may be a reason why he doesn't keep detailed studies, or even mental notes, of every hitter in the league, as many more scientific pitchers do.

"I didn't follow baseball as a kid," he confessed. "We always played. I played Little League and American Legion ball and I kept on playing, and I'm still playing.

"But I wasn't much of a fan. You know, I never got one athlete's autograph as a kid? Not one. Once we got off the field, I had other interests, like working on cars, hanging around with the guys, building tree houses, stuff like that.

"The only sports book I've ever read was a basketball book. About Bob Cousy. I did that for a book report because it was easy."

Other pitchers grew up reading about how major-league pitchers "kept a book" on hitters. By midseason, when The Bird was as famous as any pitcher in the American League, he still hadn't faced some good hitters, and things were happening so fast, he had little time to remember those he had embarrassed.

For him, the saying "ignorance is bliss" fits well.

Because he didn't know how good some hitters were, he didn't have to fear their reputations, or challenge their reputations, whichever the case may have been.

Actually, if Fred Gladding's prediction had held up, Fidrych may not have been in the majors in 1976.

"I'll be honest with you," Gladding told a sportswriter halfway through the 1976 season. "I thought he needed another year of experience. But he's got better control than he had last year. He's getting his breaking ball over more consistently.

"He's got a smooth delivery—not herky-jerky.

"He's got a good pitcher's body. He's not muscle-bound. You don't see many guys who are real thin like he is have a lot of arm trouble. It's the big fat guys—like me—who have trouble.

"What I also like is the way he grips the ball with the seams instead of across them. You get more life in the ball that way. You gotta really have a good arm to grip the ball across the seams and make it hop.

"Some pitchers can't throw that way, and others don't want to. Bird's ball sinks when he throws it with the seams. It's a moving fastball. Anytime your fastball is alive and moving, the hitters have a hard time getting wood on it."

Gladding has been around the Don Drysdales and Sandy Koufaxes, and he knew it was inevitable that The Bird's unbelievable string would come to at least a temporary halt. "He's young, he's different, and he's got a lot of baseball ahead of him," said Gladding.

Who gets the credit for his being where he is?

"He's done everything himself," the pitching coach said. "All we did was work him in gradually."

Rival manager Earl Weaver of the Baltimore Orioles, an organization that is known for its pitching heritage, said, "Fidrych is years ahead of his age. He's got some things that are just born into him. You can't acquire what he's got."

GAME PLAYED JUNE 16

KANSAS CITY	ab	r	h	bi	DETROIT	ab	r	h	bi
DNelson 2b	3	1	2	1	LeFlore cf	4	0	3	0
Otis cf	4	1	1	0	PGarcia 2b	4	0	0	0
GBrett ss	4	0	0	1	Meyer lf	4	1	1	0
Mayberry 1b	3	0	0	0	Staub rf	4	0	0	0
McRae lf	3	0	0	0	JThompson 1b	4	2	2	2
Wohlford lf	0	0	0	0	AJohnson dh	4	1	1	1
Solaita dh	3	0	0	0	ARodriguez 3b	3	0	0	0
Poquette rf	3	0	1	0	Kimm c	3	0	0	0
Quirk 3b	3	1	1	0	MStanley ph	1	0	1	1
JMartinez c	2	0	0	0	Scrivener ss	3	0	0	0
Bird p	0	0	0	0	Fidrych p	0	0	0	0
Littell p	0	0	0	0					
Hall p	0	0	0	0					
Pattin p	0	0	0	0					
Total	28	3	5	2	Total	34	4	8	4

Two out when winning run scored.

KANSAS CITY	....	100 001 010—3
DETROIT	....	010 100 002—4

E—J.Thompson, Quirk. DP—Detroit 2. LOB—Kansas City 2, Detroit 5. 2B—Otis, Quirk. HR—J. Thompson 2(6). SB—LeFlore, A.Johnson. S—J.Martinez. SF—D.Nelson.

	IP	H	R	ER	BB	SO
Bird	5	4	2	2	0	3
Littell	3	2	1	1	0	2
Hall	⅔	0	0	0	0	1
Pattin (L, 1—7)	0	2	1	1	1	0
Fidrych (W, 5—1)	9	5	3	2	2	1

T—2:08. A—21,659.

The resemblance to Harpo Marx is uncanny. But unlike the great comedian, "The Bird" talks—to baseballs, to himself, and to his teammates as he cheers them on.

They haven't drawn this many people to Tiger Stadium since Denny McLain last pitched. "The Bird" plays to packed houses.

Whatever Mark says to the ball seems to be working. It's been going pretty much where the right-hander has asked it to all season.

Fidrych has cause to smile. Not only was he the starting pitcher in this year's All-Star game, but he's up for Rookie-of-the-Year honors.

With arms flailing, "The Bird" prepares to let fly a fastball.

Besides being an extraordinary pitcher, Mark is an expert bubble blower . . .

. . . well
. . . you can't
win them all!

Detroit fans are
wild for Mark. He's
captivated the
crowd with his
skillful pitching and
his on-the-field
antics.

Sunday, June 20
AT MINNESOTA

He wasn't the same Mark Fidrych baseball had seen before when he struggled through a game with the Minnesota Twins at Metropolitan Stadium when only 11,916 showed up on a sunny Sunday afternoon.

It would be a different scene exactly one month later when over 30,000 would turn out and the Twins' management would give it a full go—complete with the release of a flock of thirteen homing pigeons and a fan in a bright yellow bird costume dancing on the Tigers' dugout roof.

In that second game against the Twins, the home team was definitely playing off The Bird's growing reputation as a flake, an unkind cut the Tigers were trying to discourage.

People who saw Fidrych pitch had mixed feelings about his silly-looking antics, which were completely alien to what they were used to from major-leaguers.

Some thought he was a flake; others wrote nasty letters to reporters who suggested such a description.

But the "flake" description was at its peak when The Bird took the mound for the June 20 game against Minnesota.

He didn't have time to worry about it, though. The Bird was wild, he got hit badly, he didn't even finish the game.

Some solid hitting by the Tigers—including a home run and four runs-batted-in by Jason Thompson—saved the day for Fidrych, and got him his fifth straight victory. But that was all there was to crow about.

The Bird didn't have it from the start. In the second inning, after the Tigers gave him a one-run lead, Fidrych got the first two Twins out, but then walked two men and gave up a single. That tied the game.

The Tigers got three more runs in the third inning, and built up the lead to 7–2 by the seventh. Yet Fidrych, who once said he'd rather pitch in a tight ballgame than with a 6–0 lead because he concentrates more, couldn't enjoy the support.

When two more walks and a double gave the Twins their third run in the eighth inning, Ralph Houk marched to the mound and replaced Fidrych with John Hiller, the team's ace relief pitcher. John saved the 7–3 victory, though Mark got the win.

In seven and a third innings, Fidrych had given

up nine hits and six walks. The latter statistic proved his undoing, and proved he was wild.

But The Bird nevertheless got the win—which proved he was definitely more pitcher than performer.

The so-called flaky baseball players over the years have added much to the lore of the game. They are fun to watch, they are unpredictable, they draw big crowds and lots of attention. But many of them also have had short careers.

The dictionary doesn't have an entry for "flake" as a person. Nobody is sure where the word came from. But there have been many players—especially pitchers—who fit the category. Pitchers seem to have the edge because they command so much attention while the game is in progress. The game is in their hands because they are the ones who have to initiate every play.

But one sportswriter theorized that pitchers have the opportunity to lead the league in flakiness because they really only play every fourth day, and they have a lot of time in between to do strange things.

One only has to take a look through baseball history to see how pitchers have monopolized the category. Sure, there was Casey Stengel, the outfielder, doffing his cap and allowing a bird to fly out of it while he was in the field one day. And some of the things Babe Ruth (who actually began his major-league career as a pitcher) did scarcely belong in the Hall of Fame.

But the Dizzies and Dazzies and the Daffies on the mound along with the Bos and the Bobos, have led the leagues over the years in doing strange things.

Like, how many players have been traded to the same team *five* times, as Bobo Newsome was during his long major-league career? That's how many times Newsome went to the Washington Senators, and how many times he was let go. The colorful Bobo, the only 200-game winner in big-league history to *lose* more times than he won, stayed around for twenty years—longer than any flake—but never more than two consecutive seasons with any one team. His longest stay was with the Tigers, but that was interrupted when he followed a twenty-one-victory season with twenty-defeats.

There were two fast-starting flakes—Bobo Holloman and Bo Belinsky—who were also fast finishers.

Holloman came up with the old St. Louis Browns in 1953, and after brooding on the bench, finally got a starting assignment. He pitched a no-hitter. But in the course of that season, the twenty-nine-year-old rookie lost his control, won only a total of three games, and disappeared into the depths of the minors.

Belinsky, many feel, sealed his own fate after stunning the baseball world with a no-hitter for the Los Angeles Angels in 1962. He became an immediate hit—on talk shows, with endorsements, with the ladies. The first thing he did after he got a large bonus for the no-hitter was to go out and buy himself a candy-apple-red Cadillac, so that he could pursue the ladies better. Belinsky unfortunately became a hit for opposing batters—he gave up 603 of them in 665 innings—and the closest he came to a winning record in any year of his eight in the majors was 9–8.

Shucks Pruett was another example.

He pitched for the old St. Louis Browns in the 1920s. He couldn't get anybody out—except Babe Ruth. He struck Ruth out ten of the thirteen times he faced him.

The exploits of Dizzy Dean have been well chronicled. The focal point of the silly St. Louis Cardinals' Gas House Gang did enough zany things to fill books, and he was hired as a broadcaster later so he could retell those stories.

But even this Hall of Famer, who was sort of an Okie version of Mark Fidrych, had a sad ending—he was hit by a line drive in an All-Star game and never was the same again.

Of all the strange things that Mark Fidrych did, however, few were contrived.

Sure, there were moments back home in Northboro where he once introduced a dance at a discothèque.

As he recalled it, "We went to this place and laid down on our backs and rolled around. The lady even introduced us and everything. She said, 'Ladies and Gentlemen, you're going to see a new dance step: The Fried Egg.'

"My buddy and I laid down on our backs and rolled around bumping into each other. It was really neat to do. The people loved it. They clapped and thought it was great.

"But the bouncer asked us to leave. I guess he didn't think it was funny."

When a reporter asked him for his favorite story, he started telling about a very plump girl, a bunch of his friends, and a camera, which he was going to allow the reporter to print until the journalist thought otherwise.

When Fidrych did make it to the Tigers' training camp, his teammates noticed he had this funny habit of poking his finger in the coin-return slots of telephones whenever he passed one.

On the first road trip with the Tigers, The Bird forgot his identification when he went to a bar in Anaheim where the Tigers stay while playing the California Angels. The bartender looked at his boyish face and refused to serve him.

The Bird sought out Tom Veryzer, his roommate, and borrowed his I.D. card. He could have done worse—say, like borrowing Willie Horton's or Ralph Houk's. But the elongated Fidrych hardly looked similar to the pudgy Veryzer.

The bartender questioned him, obviously, as he looked down at the I.D. card and looked up at Fidrych.

"What did you say your name is?" he asked.

"I'm Mark Fidrych. I play for the Detroit Tigers."

After a hearty laugh, the bartender served him.

Of course, anyone can do those things, whether he's a ballplayer or not.

It was his other habits that got people using the term "flake."

Sportswriters just weren't used to a pitcher patting the dirt on the mound into place with his hand, even if it was not his pitching hand. In fact, no one, nowhere, had seen that before. And the pitching habits—aiming the ball, loosening his arm with high windmill moves, stalking around the mound impatiently, pitching a mile a minute, talking, talking, talking—were things that major leaguers just weren't used to. Certainly, not all in one package.

At first, he offended some opposing batters. They thought he was trying to taunt them. Some kidded him and some talked back. He became the target of bench jockeys.

A few players told reporters he was "bush."

One player moved out toward the mound after him because he thought Fidrych threw at him, instead of to him, after making one of those pointing motions with the ball before he pitched.

But Fidrych came through as a pitcher, and that's the thing that bothered opponents most (though dozens of them, veterans included, kept saying he "is good for baseball").

"I think opposing batters would not get mad at him," said Eddie Matthews, the former home-run hitter who now scouts for the Milwaukee Brewers, after seeing him for the first time in the majors. "He's not like that guy in St. Louis who takes his time and tries to get people rattled. He's a young kid, he's hyper, but he's not trying to get to people."

Veteran managers such as Chuck Tanner of the Oakland Athletics marveled at his ability and dismissed his antics as just being part of The Bird. Tanner said:

"If there's one thing he's not, it's flaky. I don't know why everybody keeps printing that."

Fidrych's ability to make friends—in junior ball he once walked over to shake the hand of a pitcher who beat him in a no-hit battle—helps. His comments about opposing players such as the Yankees' All-Star catcher Thurman Munson are forgotten almost as quickly as they candidly roll off his tongue. He never means malice.

It's one thing to make a quick remark and it's another to be boastful, such as John (The Count) Montefusco was when that San Francisco Giants pitcher announced he was "going to strike out Johnny Bench [the Cincinnati Reds' slugger] four times" in their next game. That riled Bench, who ripped him for a 460-foot home run when they met.

Most of Fidrych's comments—good and bad—are centered around his own pitching.

When he talks on the mound, opposing players find humor in the situation.

Toby Harrah, the shortstop of the Texas Rangers, found it so funny that he began talking back.

"You're not going to get me out," he said.

Graig Nettles, of the New York Yankees, and Al

Bumbry, of the Baltimore Orioles, are two of the players who talked to their bats in jest when Fidrych pitched against them.

"I'm going to make sure I've got everything going for me, too," said Bumbry.

Ralph Houk told reporters he wished they would not use the word. "He's anything but flaky when he does some of those things on the mound," the manager said. "He's just being himself out there. He doesn't do it for the crowd. Even when the place is full, he doesn't even know they are there."

Fidrych himself doesn't think the description fits.

"I'm not a flake," he said. "I've always been hyper. Whatever I do, I get a bang out of it. But people can say what they want. I don't care what they call me. I'm just being me.

"Just because I do things different, or weird, that's life. A lot of people do weird things. Every pitcher gets into his own things. That's just the way I get into mine."

Virginia Fidrych, his mother, is one who worried about the stories about her son being flaky, however.

She became concerned when she first heard the phrase. She didn't know what it meant. So she approached a friend and asked.

"Your son isn't flaky," the friend said. "Don't believe any of that talk."

But Mrs. Fidrych was still worried. She thought that flaky meant he was on drugs, or something similar, she said.

But Mark maintains a natural high, without the

help of drugs. When he makes people laugh, he's just being himself. Every time an opponent gets a base hit off him, Fidrych strides off the mound and lobs the ball to the home plate umpire and asks for a new one.

"It's in my mind that that ball has a hit in it," he explained.

Of course, if the ball isn't badly damaged, the umpire will simply stick it in his pocket and toss it back into the game at a later time.

Fidrych knows that. But it doesn't bother him.

"At least I won't know that's the same ball," he points out.

GAME PLAYED JUNE 20

DETROIT	ab	r	h	bi	MINNESOTA	ab	r	h	bi
LeFlore cf	5	1	3	1	Bostock rf	4	0	2	0
Veryzer ss	4	2	2	0	Ford rf	1	0	0	0
Meyer lf	5	1	1	0	Braun dh	4	0	0	0
Staub rf	4	0	1	1	Roof ph	1	0	1	0
JThompson 1b	5	1	2	4	Carew 1b	5	0	1	0
AJohnson dh	4	1	1	0	Wynegar c	5	1	3	0
ARodriguez 3b	4	0	2	1	Cubbage 3b	2	1	0	0
PGarcia 2b	4	0	0	0	McKay ph	1	0	0	0
Kimm c	3	1	0	0	Hisle lf	3	1	0	0
Fidrych p	0	0	0	0	Brye cf	3	0	2	2
Hiller p	0	0	0	0	Terrell ss	4	0	2	1
					Randall 2b	2	0	0	0
					Kusick 1b	0	0	0	0
					Singer p	0	0	0	0
					Luebber p	0	0	0	0
					Burgmeir p	0	0	0	0
Total	38	7	12	7	Total	35	3	11	3

```
DETROIT ............................................... 013 100 200—7
MINNESOTA ........................................... 010 001 010—3
```

DP—Detroit 1. LOB—Detroit 7, Minnesota 12. 2B—A.Rodriguez, LeFlore, Brye, Wynegar. HR—J.Thompson (8). SF—Staub.

	IP	H	R	ER	BB	SO
Fidrych (W, 6–1)	7 1/3	9	3	3	6	2
Hiller	1 2/3	2	0	0	1	3
Singer (L, 5–3)	7	10	7	7	1	1
Luebber	1 2/3	2	0	0	0	2
Burgmeir	1/3	0	0	0	0	0

Save—Hiller (6). HBP—by Singer. Balk—Singer. T—2:40. A—11,916.

Thursday, June 24
AT BOSTON

As the Bird was breezing through the first few innings against the Red Sox in Boston—the team that had become his personal nemesis—a fan spotted Virginia Fidrych with her husband and children in the stands and hollered out: "Hey, lady, what did you feed that kid—birdseed?"

The Tigers hadn't been at home in several days, so it was difficult for The Bird to test his true popularity. The game the following Monday against the New York Yankees, on national television, would be the real barometer. But the fact that even fans on the road were beginning to get caught up in Fidrych's wonderful whirl showed what direction he was headed if he kept on winning.

Fidrych wanted to beat the Red Sox badly. "They burned me three times," he said. "Once here [the game almost exactly a month before] and twice in spring training when I was trying to make the team." The Red Sox had also beaten the Tigers five straight in regular season, which is one reason Manager Ralph Houk had recently listed Mark for his starter with just three days rest. In earlier games, Houk had given his newcomer four to five days off between starts.

Fidrych almost let them down in Boston.

After pitching three tight opening innings, he allowed Cecil Cooper to lead off the fourth with a booming triple, helped along by the right fielder's misplay of the ball. Cooper scored on the next out. Then Fred Lynn and Carl Yastrzemski smacked consecutive home runs.

"It looked like Rocket City," Fidrych recalled later. "I had a sore neck from turning around and watching the ball fly over the fence. I didn't think I was going to make it."

In the stands, Mrs. Fidrych was tearing apart another set of rosary beads, her third string of the young season.

Manager Houk showed his concern. He went to the mound to settle the rookie and told him if he held the Red Sox during the inning, the Tigers would get him some runs.

A whole season—indeed, a whole legend—could have been left right there on the pitcher's mound at Fenway Park if Houk had pulled his rookie, or if Fidrych stayed in and absorbed the loss. He would have been a mere mortal with a 6–2 record. That game, coupled with his mediocre (for him) showing in Minnesota, would not have gotten

ABC-television excited about doing his game the following Monday.

Other things would have fallen by the wayside, too.

But The Bird buckled down.

The team got him the runs he needed—and then some—as Rusty Staub and Jason Thompson began clouting the ball. Five more runs were added to an earlier one, giving The Bird the support he needed. He responded by shutting out Boston's big hitters for the rest of the game.

With two men out and one on base for Boston in the ninth inning, third-baseman Aurelio Rodriguez dropped an easy pop fly ball that should have ended the game.

Many young pitchers would have been shattered at that point. After all, that meant Fidrych would have to face the dangerous Rico Petrocelli, with runners on base.

Petrocelli is made to order for Boston's short right-field fence, and a homer would have tied the game.

But instead of being rattled, The Bird dashed over to third base, where he consoled Rodriguez with a pat on the back and told him not to worry.

Then he went back to the pitcher's mound and struck Petrocelli out on three pitches.

"You might have thought the kid would go to pieces, but he struck him out," said Houk. "He's got great concentration. That's the biggest thing I've ever seen him do."

The strikeout gave Fidrych a 6–3 victory. Despite the geography of the ballpark, he gave up only seven hits.

The result of the victory, besides a 7–1 record for Fidrych, was a new wave of interest.

It's hard to say where it started.

Darrell Johnson, the Boston manager, had a lot to do with it. The fact that he was going to be the manager of the American League All-Stars for the July 13 game in Philadelphia prompted the writers to ask him of Fidrych's chances.

Johnson thought highly of the rookie, and even if his team was in the same division, battling the Tigers for a second-place finish that they could not have thought of without Fidrych, he was generous enough to tout the Tiger rookie.

"Yes, he has a chance [to make the All-Star team]," the manager said after the game.

"Make that a good chance. The kid has good stuff. He's shown me he knows how to pitch and has a lot of guts." Johnson's chief scout, Frank Malzone, called Fidrych "the best pitcher in baseball."

Johnson discounted the "colorful stuff," preferring to dwell on the talents that gave Fidrych seven complete games in eight starts, a 2.19 earned-run average and the 7–1 record. In almost every game, he had to pitch himself out of a jam. Nothing was coming easy. Nothing was undramatic, either.

But Johnson was selling Fidrych short when he dismissed the colorful aspect of the rookie.

By now, *Sports Illustrated*, *People* magazine, *Newsweek*, the *Wall Street Journal* and others who were not looking for the ordinary, run-of-the-mill rookie began paying closer attention to Mark Fidrych.

The *Journal* put Fidrych on its front page.

The wire-service roundups were putting his feats at the top of their stories. In New York City and other key media locations, Fidrych was beginning to get top billing.

Mary McGrory, the national syndicated political columnist, would soon do a column on him, suggesting that if he weren't so young, he'd make a good running-mate for Jimmy Carter's Presidential bid. "Mark Fidrych is a super-kid, and I'm sure the Democrats would nominate him for Vice-President if they could. Some perspective is needed. Mark Fidrych talks to baseballs. Jimmy Carter talks to God. . . ."

And when Fidrych finally was named to the All-Star squad a few days later, he got bigger play in some newspapers than their own local stars.

The important point here is charisma, that much-bandied-about word that separates the Joe Namaths from the Joe Schmooes. The general (non-sports) writers will flock to someone who has more to offer than a ton of statistics. The Babe Ruths and the Muhammad Alis live on. What happened to the Walter Johnsons and the Joe Louises?

America needed a Mark Fidrych as much as Detroit did.

He was a free spirit, unconcerned with dress codes, money, materialistic things.

The more reporters got close to him, the more they liked him—and the stories he generated.

After the game in Boston, his mother was determined to get into the dressing room to see him.

"But you can't," the guard said, explaining that the players weren't dressed yet.

"Why not? I've seen that kid in the nude before," she answered.

Meanwhile, Mark's dad was sneaking in, posing as a reporter, much to his son's chagrin.

Afterward, Virginia Fidrych was seen trying to climb under a fence that separates the players from fans. On an earlier trip she had tried to get on the team bus to get autographs. The Bird wanted to crawl under the seat.

The team would be in Boston for a few more days, then head home to Detroit for the televised game with the Yankees. In no time at all, there would be no privacy for Fidrych, whether it was invasions by his mother, reporters, or fans.

The Bird had gone public, whether he liked it or not.

Fidrych's life would be unveiled. *People* magazine sent a reporter and photographer team to his colorless apartment in the Detroit suburb of Southgate, a workingman's community. They learned the little details that make magazine stories work for the non-sports fans, facts such as that his bedroom consisted only of the bare essentials, if that. A tablecloth covered his window.

But The Bird cooperated beautifully.

"Why should I get drapes," he said. "I ain't got a wife."

Other reporters learned about his hyped-up nature—to the point where he admitted that he had to pump his own gas most of the times when he pulled into a filling station because he couldn't stand waiting around.

He talked of going home at night to a sink full of dirty dishes—all four of them.

He lived in this day and age without a television set, his main entertainment being a stereo he was given for appearing on a sports show.

While other players talked about stocks and bonds, he talked about the possibility of going home and working for Pierce Oil and Gas during the winter. A year before, he made $2 an hour there.

And when other players drove up in flashy Buicks and Chryslers and Cadillacs, he pulled in the stadium parking lot with his dented Dodge Colt, a luxury he afforded himself after his '69 Chevy obviously wasn't going to make it to Florida for spring training.

Did he dream of Buicks or Caddies?

Heavens no, he said seriously. He was looking forward to getting a pickup truck—a beat-up one at that.

He began getting gifts in the mail.

A stuffed toy bird. A bird cage. One person sent him flowers.

His mail piled up higher than anyone's on the team.

Dozens of letters poured in daily, some asking for autographs, others asking for dates. Somebody invited him to a high school graduation barbecue.

Teammates began clearing his corner in the clubhouse to make way for hordes of reporters after games.

He accommodated the media to the end. Once in a while, he might say, "Excuse me, I wanna get a beer," then sprint across the clubhouse in the nude, grab a beer and sprint back to continue the conversation. *Sports Illustrated*'s man noticed him with a cup of milk on the rocks in one hand, and a succession of beers to chase it down.

To get their stories, though, they had to wait for him to applaud his teammates for their individual plays, sometimes grabbing and introducing a player to a press corps that had known that player for years.

He wondered out loud about getting a "big head," and his father would call as the momentum built up to make sure "you keep your head screwed on."

He answered questions candidly.

"Mark, what do you think of Detroit?"

"I like it all right. I haven't gotten beat up yet," he'd say, and everybody had a good laugh.

He made it very clear that there was nothing wrong with his lifestyle—because it was his own.

"If people don't like me, he's not a good guy,"

he'd say, then invent some language of his own. "They'd be *hypocritics*."

Meanwhile in Detroit the lines were forming at the ticket windows at Tiger Stadium and everyone was awaiting his return home.

Businesses began flourishing in the carnival atmosphere that was building.

"Bird's the Word" was being pressed on T-shirts as fast as entrepreneurs could make them. "Bird" buttons were manufactured by the thousands for sale outside Tiger Stadium. "Go Bird Go" bumper stickers made their first appearances.

Even Detroit's two major newspapers began working on an "iron off" decal that could be pressed from the back page of the paper onto a T-shirt. One paper did it so fast, they turned The Bird into a southpaw.

It seemed that every writer in the city was getting The Bird into the lead of his or her story. Radio announcers were asked questions about him on their talk shows and popped Bird stories to their audiences.

A national wire service wrote a feature on him that was carried by almost all of its subscribers, coast to coast.

Baseball hadn't seen the likes of it since . . . well, maybe never.

GAME PLAYED JUNE 24

DETROIT	ab	r	h	bi	BOSTON	ab	r	h	bi
LeFlore cf	5	0	2	0	Cooper dh	4	1	1	0
Veryzer ss	5	0	0	0	DGriffin 2b	3	0	0	1
Oglivie rf	5	1	1	0	RiMiller ph	1	0	0	0
Staub dh	4	2	3	1	Doyle 2b	0	0	0	0
JThompson 1b	3	2	2	2	Lynn cf	4	1	1	1
AJohnson lf	4	0	1	1	Ystrmski 1b	3	1	2	1
ARodriguez 3b	4	1	2	1	Rice lf	3	0	0	0
PGarcia 2b	3	0	0	1	Fisk c	4	0	1	0
Kimm c	3	0	1	0	DEvans rf	4	0	1	0
Fidrych p	0	0	0	0	Petrocelli 3b	4	0	0	0
					Burleson ss	3	0	1	0
					Wise p	0	0	0	0
					Cleveland p	0	0	0	0
Total	36	6	12	6	Total	33	3	7	3

DETROIT	....	000 103 020—6
BOSTON	....	000 300 000—3

E—Cleveland, A.Rodriguez. DP—Detroit 2, Boston 2. LOB—Detroit 6, Boston 5. 2B—J.Thompson, Staub. 3B—A.Rodriguez, Cooper. HR—J.Thompson (9), Lynn (5), Yastrzemski (13). SF—P.Garcia.

	IP	H	R	ER	BB	SO
Fidrych (W, 7–1)	9	7	3	3	2	4
Wise (L, 5–5)	5	9	4	4	1	2
Cleveland	4	3	2	2	1	3

T—2:31. A—26,293.

Monday, June 28
VS. THE NEW YORK YANKEES

There is a certain homage paid to the New York Yankees that is unique in American sports. For one thing, they wear pinstripes on their uniforms, which is typical of those Wall Street brokers in their pinstripe suits. There is the Yankees' image of victory and success and gobs of money, all of which are very American.

The Yankees traditionally play the game straight —with power and pitching and few gimmicks. So it was no wonder that the New Yorkers' All-Star catcher, Thurman Munson, would suggest that some of Mark Fidrych's antics were "bush."

To which The Bird, in all his lack of reverence, asked who Thurman Munson was, and what he had done lately. When he was told that Munson was the star Yankee catcher, even though he didn't play because of an injury, he said:

"Well, *bleep* him."

Here was a rookie so raw that he told a reporter he had never heard of Roger Maris. When somebody mentioned Babe Ruth, The Bird asked: "What has he done lately? He's gone. *Bleep* him."

Facing the Yankees for the first time in his career, Fidrych refused to respect the fact that the Yankees of 1976 were a revived version of the old championship-style teams that won pennants and World Series in bunches. The new version consisted of one of the best hitting teams in baseball, a squad deep in pitching, and a team that had an eleven-game lead over the Detroit Tigers, who had yet to play .500 baseball despite The Bird's heroics.

But The Bird had his strengths, too.

The ticket windows at Tiger Stadium closed down almost an hour before the 8:40 P.M. starting time. Left on the streets surrounding the old ballpark were an estimated 10,000 fans who had come to get tickets, but were turned away unless they wanted obstructed seats.

Of those who did cram into the ballpark, it was as if the ticket sellers had given them voice tests. It was one of the loudest groups ever assembled, almost to the person there to cheer Mark Fidrych. He owned the audience.

They cheered his every move—before, during, and after the game, even though the game turned out to be anticlimactic.

The fans came early, and hollered every time he threw a ball in the warm-ups. You'd think he was striking out Mantle, Ruth, and Gehrig in order.

The fact that national television was there to incorporate his feats into the lore of baseball, and that about 9 million households—as television likes to measure its impact—would see the game in all but six states and the Detroit area, added to the importance. It was the eighth such game in ABC-TV's 1976 Monday-night series, and the one ABC was most excited about.

The Bird's arrival on the mound after the national anthem was again reason for a rousing cheer. The Yankees stood stunned as they listened to tens of thousands of rival fans scream as the Tiger pitcher went through his unorthodox method of tidying up the dirt around the mound.

There were some clutches of fans yelling, "Go, Bird, go! Go, Bird, go!" but nothing like what would be coming.

The sign wavers were also in style, with "GO GET 'EM, BIRD" and "DROP A BIG ONE ON THEM, BIRD."

New York writers traveling with the team learned for the first time that this was The Bird, not "Big Bird" as they had been writing.

For the next few innings, they had that pressed upon their eardrums. "Go, Bird, go!"

The Bird went right after Mickey Rivers, who came into the game with a twenty-game hitting streak. Mark got him to ground out, and held him hitless for the night.

The hyped-up Bird was wiggling his knees, loosening his wrist, and taking deep breaths with almost every pitch. There was no question he was going to concentrate on this game, no matter how little he admitted he knew about the Yankees. After one man got on and another was out, Mark went after gigantic Chris Chambliss, the Yanks' first baseman, and got him on a strikeout—with a fine final pitch that broke so well Chambliss didn't even take his bat off his shoulder.

The Tigers got two runs in the bottom of the first —thanks to a homer by Rusty Staub, who hadn't had one in over six weeks. Not surprisingly, Staub had been telling reporters how well the team rallies behind Fidrych when he pitches.

The Yankees came back with a run in the second when their catcher, Elrod Hendricks, slammed a home run into the lower deck of right field.

But it was all The Bird after that.

He settled down and kept the Yankees in line, not allowing any of them to get past second base. Rivers, the speedster with the hitting streak, ground out four straight times as Fidrych made almost a special case of him. Each time Rivers came up, The Bird flexed his fingers, and sometimes his knees, and once pointed the ball forward as if to aim it.

In the broadcasting booth, ABC-TV's funnyman, Bob Uecker, was having a field day trying to describe him.

"He's tall, lean, and has web feet," said the former major-league catcher.

But Uecker also marveled about how Fidrych would not allow himself to fall behind the batters in the early going. Fidrych wouldn't walk a man all night.

ABC timed Fidrych's pitches early and late in the game. Both times the technician came up with a fast 93 mph figure.

He was concentrating so intensely he hardly noticed the crowd that was chanting "Go, Bird, go! Go, Bird, go!" half the night. Much of that time, the crowd was on its feet.

If he was listening to anybody, it was himself. He was chatting up a storm.

At one point, Graig Nettles, one of the Yankees' heavier hitters, turned his back on the mound as he was fixing the batting box with his feet. Fidrych had been zeroing the ball at the strike zone, and it came across as if The Bird were giving him a voodoo sign, shaking the ball at his back.

Whatever Fidrych was doing, he was doing it right.

The Yankees couldn't catch him, his teammates supported with three more runs, and he had a well-deserved 5–1 victory. The crowd couldn't cheer enough. The Bird flew off the mound as if he had just won the World Series. He hugged teammates, grounds keepers, anyone in sight. He waved his cap, hugged his head, pranced around—and shook everyone's hand.

The game was over, but the crowd had not had enough. A light rain was falling.

Fidrych was kept around for a television interview with Uecker in the Tiger dugout, and that in itself may have been the thing that touched off a baseball phenomenon. He was cheered loudly while standing there, and he waved to the cheering sections.

As Uecker and Fidrych waited for the camera to come on, The Bird looked up to the booth where ABC's Bob Prince and Warner Wolf were wrapping up the game action.

"Where's Curt Gowdy?" The Bird asked.

"This is ABC," replied Uecker.

"Well, where's Curt Gowdy?" The Bird repeated.

"I'm sorry, he's not here," said Uecker.

"He does Monday-night baseball," said The Bird.

"You got the wrong network, Bird," said Uecker. Gowdy was NBC's Saturday "Game of the Week" man.

When their interview finally was over, and thousands of fans standing idly by as far away as the center-field bleachers despite the light rain, The Bird began to leave, then suddenly turned back to Uecker.

"Where's my gift? I thought I got a gift on national TV," he said.

Again, Uecker had to explain that must be some other network.

But the fans may have taken The Bird's cue when he turned and came back. The fans yelling "Go, Bird, go!" changed their chant. Now thousands began yelling "We want The Bird! We want The Bird!"

They refused to leave. The chants persisted.

Baseball players don't take encores, especially after they head for the clubhouse. But the fans wouldn't leave. They continued to chant in unison. The chant became deafening, and it could be heard all the way to the clubhouse.

In what may have been his greatest move since coming to the big leagues, Fidrych decided to acknowledge them. He did it his way, bringing out several of the Tigers with him. He'd accept their cheers if he could share them with his teammates.

The crowd went wild when he appeared, his feet only clad in baseball stockings and his moppy hair flopping all over. A fan with the sign "Mark, We Love You" tried to lift it so The Bird could see it.

He didn't need to. He could tell the love was there. He waved and smiled.

Rusty Staub, one of the players who went back to the field with The Bird, tried to put it all in perspective. Staub had played in Houston when the Astrodome was opened, in Montreal when that city joyously welcomed major-league baseball, and in New York when baseball's zaniest fans—the Mets followers—saw their former ragtags with a pennant. Mets fans tried to rip Shea Stadium apart in the process.

"He's the most exciting thing I've ever seen in a city," Staub said. "He brings electricity to the game for the players and the fans."

Bill Freehan, the old veteran of many Tiger battles, including the 1968 World Series, admitted he had more calls and bought more tickets for this one game—52 in all—than he ever did for the Series it-self. His phone began jumping off the hook at eight o'clock that morning.

Upstairs in the television booth, where veteran announcer Bob Prince, mostly a National Leaguer throughout his career, said he had to admit: "I never saw anything like this, he is such a refreshingly beautiful young man."

Fidrych had gotten more cheers after the game than most players do in a lifetime. He'd gotten more during the game than most top pitchers do in a season.

He had become more than a celebrity. He became a national symbol for the game. Before the night was over, his name was etched into baseball history forever.

But could he handle it?

Ralph Houk, the Yankee manager when that team was winning World Series back in the early 1960s, said he had never seen anything like it. He openly and proudly said that it was The Bird—not the Yankees, not the Tigers, not TV—that drew the rousing crowd. He said it was Fidrych who turned them on once they settled in their seats, for what little time they stayed seated.

"I don't think there's any question, he drew this crowd," the manager said. "I expected him to be a success, but I never would have believed it could happen this fast.

"I don't think even Walter Johnson started this fast."

No, Walter Johnson didn't. At age twenty-one, the immortal right-hander turned in a 13–25 record. Warren Spahn was five years away from the majors at twenty-one. Sandy Koufax was struggling to get starts at twenty-one and would need five more years to really come around. He wasn't a crowd drawer until he was twenty-eight.

About the only player in years who had started that fast was Whitey Ford of the Yankees, who ironically was the ace of several of Houk's staffs. In 1950, Ford came up late and compiled a 9–1 record with a 2.81 earned-run average. But that was with one of the greatest of all Yankee teams.

Fidrych now stood at 8–1, with a league-leading 2.05 earned-run average.

But the Fidrych phenomenon was not just baseball statistics. Rather it included the crowds he had turned on.

The way he could pick up the tempo in the late innings when he should have been getting tired, the way he could protect a tight lead week after week without failing, the way he could turn off all that drama in the crowd he created—that's what it was all about.

Yes, he admitted, he had butterflies at the start, and again near the end.

"As the game wore on I got over them," he explained. "But they came back again in the ninth. I have to keep my mind on the game. I have to keep driving myself when my ball is slowing down."

Yes, he kept up a constant chatter.

"I just kept saying, 'Let it flow,'" he said of his conversations with the ball which were more in evidence than ever. "I told myself, I gotta throw hard . . . I gotta throw hard.

"In the ninth, I just kept telling myself, 'Three more outs and the game is over . . . come on, just three more outs!'

"I got to do that, that's just my way of keeping my mind on the game. If I don't, I relax and my body seems to slow down. I've got to concentrate on every pitch.

"The adrenalin was flowing out there, though. The people really get me up."

As he spoke, he wrote the crowd figure on a strange little newspaper clipping that he pinned to the top of his locker, alongside a crayon drawing of a bird that someone sent him.

The picture on the clipping, from his paper in Northboro, showed an eighty-year-old Oriental woman throwing a shot put. The caption said she could put it about fifteen feet.

He wouldn't explain the significance, but the figures spoke for themselves. They were from the home games that the Tigers had him on the mound as a starter.

The numbers in order told a story:

14,583
17,894
21,659
36,377
47,855

The total was already 138,398, the average

27,680—almost twice what the Tigers had averaged the year before.

"One of a kind" the caption said.

In the days that followed, everyone wanted Mark Fidrych. He was front-page stuff on the Detroit *News* the next afternoon.

"TIGERS FLY HIGH WITH 'BIRD' " the *News* headline blared. The story and seven-column picture took up more than a quarter of the top of the page.

The Detroit *Free Press* gave him almost all the first sports page.

"GO, BIRD, GO! FIDRYCH KILLS NY, 5–1" said the *Free Press*'s eight-column banner. A couple of days later, he would be on the front page of that paper, too, with a complete detailed story of his life.

Across the state, his legend grew.

"'BIRD' MESMERIZES MICHIGAN," said an eight-column headline in the Grand Rapids *Press*.

With the Tigers home for two more games against the Yankees, Fidrych became a marked man.

A stack of telegrams, letters, and telephone messages six inches deep awaited him the next day.

Interviewers, agents, promoters, long-lost relatives, old friends tried to reach him. Newspapers from Washington to San Diego, and television and radio announcers from San Antonio to Denver, tried to reach him.

On Tuesday, he was besieged. By Wednesday, his eyes were darkened.

He at one point just fell back into a soft chair

in the Tigers' interview lounge and let the flood-gates open. He couldn't move anyway, so he submitted to a group interview.

No, he didn't think he was flaky.

Yes, he worked in a gas station and would like to again some day.

No, he didn't have a telephone in his apartment; if he did, he'd never have a moment of peace.

Yes, agents were calling him.

No, he didn't want anyone to represent him; only he, he said, knew his true worth, and could negotiate it.

Yes, kids are coming over to his apartment now that they know who he is; and yes, he gives them autographs though he wished they wouldn't come so early.

No, he's not going to conform and wear clothes that others want him to, though, "I have to wear good clothes now when I travel."

Yes, he thought he deserved some time of his own, that his "job" should not be treated any differently from that of the guy who works eight hours a day.

No, no, no, you reporters can't come over to the apartment for exclusive interviews.

But he did have time for the autograph hounds out on the field before game time, and he politely tried to acknowledge the well-wishers. He signed furiously, a dozen a minute or better.

He took the time to pose with the promoters of the Broadway play *Damn Yankees*, about a mythical Joe Hardy who came out of nowhere and almost single-handedly won the pennant from the Yankees for his down-trodden, last-place team.

Joe Hardy had to take his orders from a satanic figure, and he became a beaten man who gave it all up and disappeared.

Fidrych stayed on the scene, however, trying to fend off the forces of change.

Meanwhile, back home in Northboro, there was some concern as to whether he could do it.

The Fidrych family, too, was full of excitement the day after the game. Mark's pediatrician called Virginia Fidrych and reminded her how difficult a time she had had with her cesarean operation when Mark was born and how it was worth it now. Mrs. Fidrych hadn't heard from the doctor in years.

People kept visiting all day long, and the telephone was in use constantly till late in the afternoon. One caller was a man from Texas who knew Mark in the minors. Another was a Puerto Rican man who begged for a chance to let his family come over and meet the family that brought Mark Fidrych into the world. Mark, who called home regularly, didn't have a chance.

People all meant well. Kids shot off fireworks.

The pet parakeet—Angel, which used to be Mrs. Fidrych's nickname for Mark—didn't get a moment's rest.

The Fidrych's wondered what it would all do to their son. "I worry about him," Virginia Fidrych said. "Sometimes I sit down and cry 'cause I don't want him to get his arm hurt."

She almost started to cry when she said it.

But The Bird was not concerned, other than being much in need of a good night's sleep.

He went back to his "job" as usual, saying in the aftermath of triumph, "I haven't woken up yet."

"I'm just loving it," he said. "I'm just loving it."

GAME PLAYED JUNE 28

NEW YORK	ab	r	h	bi		DETROIT	ab	r	h	bi
Rivers cf	4	0	0	0		LeFlore cf	3	1	2	0
RWhite lf	4	0	2	0		Veryzer ss	4	2	1	0
CMay dh	4	0	1	0		Staub rf	4	1	1	3
Chambliss 1b	4	0	0	0		AJohnson dh	4	0	1	1
GNettles 3b	4	0	2	0		JThompson 1b	4	0	0	0
Gamble rf	4	0	1	0		ARodriguez 3b	3	1	1	1
Hendricks c	4	1	1	1		MStanley lf	3	0	0	0
Randolph 2b	3	0	0	0		PGarcia 2b	3	0	0	0
Mason ss	3	0	0	0		Kimm c	3	0	0	0
Holtzman p	0	0	0	0		Fidrych p	0	0	0	0
Total	34	1	7	1		Total	31	5	6	5

```
NEW YORK .................................. 010 000 000—1
DETROIT ..................................... 200 000 12x—5
```

E—Randolph. LOB—New York 6, Detroit 3. 2B—R.White 2, A.Johnson. HR—Staub (4), Hendricks (3), A.Rodriguez (5). SB—LeFlore 2.

	IP	H	R	ER	BB	SO
Holtzman (L, 5—6)	8	6	5	5	1	2
Fidrych (W, 8—1)	9	7	1	1	0	2

T—1:51. A—47,855.

Saturday, July 3
VS. BALTIMORE

It's one thing for a rookie pitcher to draw 50,-
000 fans to his next start. But it's an entirely different situation when he draws 80,000. But that's
what happened when The Bird's would-be start
in Baltimore suddenly got changed at the last
minute because of a rainout, and the Tigers decided to hold him a day later to pitch in Detroit
instead.

Some 30,000 people showed up in Baltimore
when they thought he would start. But 51,032 got
a chance to see him in person at Tiger Stadium
the next night, and he was his same old self.

The Orioles only once got a rally going and
that was in the fourth inning when Paul Blair
walked, Bobby Grich singled, and Reggie Jackson loaded the bases on an infield grounder.

The Bird shifted gears, became aroused and

struck out the next two batters and got the third on an infield out. He had three runs behind him at the time, and that was all he needed, though Jason Thompson rewarded him with a fourth when he socked a ball off the roof in right field.

Fidrych gave up only four hits, several of which were nullified by the way he pitched to succeeding batters and the way his infielders continued to react by making tough plays on lead base runners.

The Bird was at his peak this night.

The fans kept him there—before, during, and after the game.

Before the game, Joe Falls of the Detroit *Free Press* wrote: "Saturday night will be the greatest happening around here since last Monday night."

Maybe it was a toss-up.

Almost 100,000 fans showed up for the two games, and the Baltimore game may have had an edge in noise, if not excitement.

Count the 30,000 fans Fidrych lured to the ballpark in Baltimore and it made him responsible for 130,000 fans within a six-day span.

The Bird was making headlines for the crowds he was drawing as much as he was for his pitching, which happened to be superb.

For the record, he had been named American League Player of the Month for his June efforts —a month in which he was 6–0 on the mound with a sparkling 1.99 earned-run average. An upstate New York belt company also awarded him its prestigious Hickok Professional Athlete of the

Month award. He was leading the league in earned-run average, had a seven-game winning streak going, and was close to the top with his 9–1 overall record.

But what everyone talked about was the crowds.

"Mickey Mantle used to draw crowds," said Ralph Houk, "but I've never seen a rookie do anything like this. I don't think I've ever enjoyed anything like this in my life."

The fact that Fidrych may have been helping the manager save his job—there were rumors that he was under pressure after two last-place seasons —may have influenced Houk's enthusiasm. But the manager was smiling, and very sincere. He hadn't had many things to smile about in two years. But he could see the true value of Fidrych to the team.

"This stirs me up. It's gotta stir up the players. I wanted him to win so darn bad. The kid's so energetic, so enthused. Everything goes together."

The front office of the Tigers was just as enthused.

Ticket sales were going so well that one Bird game would hardly be over when the calls for tickets to his next game would begin.

The Bird would be held for the following Friday night, when the Tigers were again at home. There was no way the Tigers would pitch him on Wednesday—even with the full three days' rest —when they could have him at home.

It was just common sense.

Perhaps visiting ballplayer Reggie Jackson, with the Orioles after leading Oakland to three straight pennants, had used his past experience when he remarked that the public's attraction to Fidrych would wane eventually.

"He'll last [as a pitcher]," said Jackson, "but the fling won't. Everybody has their day. I saw Vida Blue do it. Even super-superstars go out once in a while."

But The Bird had one advantage over Vida Blue, the Oakland pitcher who won twenty-four games, was the league's Most Valuable Player and won the Cy Young award all at age twenty-two—his first full season in the majors. Blue, by his own admission, didn't want the notoriety that went with his pitching success.

Fidrych, on the other hand, didn't seem to understand all the fuss being made over him. Maybe he thought fans treated everyone this way when they won.

Blue wanted to burn up a stack of his fan mail one night as a personal revolt against the pressure. Fidrych as yet hadn't related the letters to his success, and wasn't that concerned with them anyway. He read his letters, and that was the end of them.

The Tigers could not think in long-range terms about their star pitcher. He was hot on the mound, as well as at the box office, and winning is just as much a part of the game as drawing crowds.

The Tigers weren't the only ones trying to get him to the mound so he would draw crowds.

Everybody was.

It had begun with NBC television, when that

network tried to get Ralph Houk to rearrange his pitching order so that Fidrych would pitch on a Saturday when the NBC-TV people had their "Game of the Week" feature. The pitching rotation would allow NBC to have Fidrych for a "Game of the Week" in late July, but that wasn't enough. Twice NBC suggested The Bird pitch on a Saturday afternoon once he became a hot television personality.

When NBC finally did get him, they began advertising "Mark (The Bird) Fidrych versus the Cleveland Indians" in their promos.

NBC wasn't alone in trying to get the Tigers to change their pitching order. ABC, whose ratings got a big boost when he pitched that Monday against the New York Yankees, were at the Tigers' door again, suggesting another Fidrych versus the Yankees game in early August.

The Tigers answered ABC with a flat no. Enough is enough.

So much for television.

The people who stood the most to gain by his appearances were the owners of the other American League teams. The Bird was obviously the hottest attraction they had among the twelve teams.

Before the Baltimore game in Detroit, it seemed that the schedule would allow The Bird to pitch on a Tuesday night in Arlington Stadium, home of the Texas Rangers.

When that rumor got around, ticket sales for Tuesday zoomed. He already had drawn 32,678 to an earlier Rangers' game in early June, and he was almost totally unknown then.

When it was decided he would pitch on a previous Saturday in Detroit, thus wiping out a Tuesday possibility in Texas but making Wednesday a likely date, ticket sales for the Wednesday game zoomed.

The switchboard was lighting up at Arlington Stadium on July 4 like a tree at Christmastime.

The Texas Rangers management hadn't had that kind of reaction since 1973, when they signed a Texas high school wonder to a contract with a $125,000 bonus. Eighteen-year-old David Clyde, fresh out of graduation exercises, drew 113,000 fans in his first four starts, thus repaying the bonus over and over again—before slipping into the minors.

The Tigers tried to be fair to everybody, which wasn't easy. Since they were not that involved in a pennant race, and since their pitching staff wasn't solid, Ralph Houk could shuffle people around a bit.

But the basic realities of sound business practice tempted the Tigers to pitch him at home every chance they got.

The average seat at Tiger Stadium goes for about $3. Individual seats range from $1.50 to $4.50. Add the dollar each fan spends, on the average, buying items from the concessions stands and you have a total of $4 per person in the stadium. Multiply that times the 50,000 seats that

Fidrych filled, and you're talking about a $200,000 gate.

Have him do it three times in a row, and the figure speaks for itself.

In 1975, the Tigers averaged 14,390 fans. The Bird never had a crowd below that.

The American League rule states that visiting teams get 20 percent of the total gate from their hosts.

Three times in his first six road games, he topped 30,000. In another game, he drew over 25,000.

One of those games was against the Minnesota Twins, which saturated the Twin Cities area with newspaper ads ("THE BIRD" WILL PITCH AGAINST THE TWINS) and radio and television plugs. The Twins had not advertised an incoming drawing card since 1968, when Denny McLain of the Tigers was the man of the hour.

McLain, one should note, was going for thirty victories, an unprecedented feat in the previous three decades, and he was with an exciting, pennant-chasing team.

Fidrych wound up drawing 30,425 to Metropolitan Stadium in Bloomington, Minnesota. That was 6,000 more fans than showed up at one of those lucrative jacket days, which until now had topped the individual attendance figures for the Twins in the first half of 1976. The Twins expected only 20,000 for The Bird.

The day after Fidrych pitched, attendance fell to 9,000, which was closer to the Twins' norm.

"Half a dozen other clubs have called to see if he would be pitching when we played them," said Campbell about one week after the All-Star game. "Hell, if he was on some other team coming to Detroit, I would be calling, too.

"That's just good business practice. Their fans all want to know if he's going to pitch there. It's unbelievable how much interest there is in him.

"I've told the other teams we've got him pitching in a rotation and he's going to continue to take his regular turn.

"As I understand it, Ralph Houk likes to pitch him every fourth day for a couple of turns, then give him an extra day off in between starts."

The schedule worked out nicely as Fidrych wound up pitching in Detroit for a game, and drew 44,000.

But his interest grew nationally, even if the Tigers preferred to pitch him at home whenever possible.

A fan in California wired the Tigers for the exact date of The Bird's next appearance in Oakland so he could buy a large block of tickets. The Tigers themselves got open-ended orders—"Here's $14, send me four tickets the next time The Bird goes."

And for those who missed out when "Birdomania" was at its peak, there were plenty of scalpers. So many, in fact, that the Detroit City Council adopted and put into effect a new ordinance banning the sale of tickets on public property. That didn't stop scalpers, though. Seven of them were arrested before the next Tiger game that Fidrych pitched.

And what was Fidrych's reaction to all this?

Here was a player who would draw 330,000 fans in his first nine home games. That total was nearly a third of the draw for the Tigers' entire 1975 home season of seventy-four dates.

He stood a chance, before the season was over, of topping the entire 1975 draws of the Chicago White Sox and the Minnesota Twins.

In fifteen games, home and away, he drew a half-million fans. The previous year, the American League as a whole drew 13 million to about nine hundred dates.

In six and a half years, the Tigers had drawn over 50,000 fans on eleven different occasions, mostly in the heat of pennant races or at special promotions, such as jacket days. With no promotions (well, there was one Windsor Night, honoring the Canadian city), Fidrych had drawn two of those 50,000 crowds. (To which Lew Matlin, of the Tigers' promotion office, remarked, "We had our greatest Windsor Night ever!")

Fidrych with his $16,000 annual salary didn't blink. He didn't make a sound about money except when reporters asked him.

Manager Houk appreciated his attitude.

"I've just told him to be himself," said Houk, "but I wanted him to concentrate on pitching the nights he was supposed to pitch."

One rival manager, Earl Weaver of the Baltimore Orioles, mentioned on a trip into Detroit:

"So he's supposed to be crazy, eh? All I know is that he's already writing down the attendance figures in front of his locker. So how crazy can he be?"

GAME PLAYED JULY 3

BALTIMORE	ab	r	h	bi		DETROIT	ab	r	h	bi
Bumbry cf	3	0	1	0		LeFlore cf	4	1	1	0
Blair cf	1	0	0	0		Veryzer ss	3	1	1	0
Muser lf	1	0	1	0		Staub rf	4	1	1	3
Grich 2b	4	0	1	0		AJohnson dh	4	0	1	0
ReJackson rf	4	0	0	0		JThompson 1b	3	1	1	1
LMay 1b	4	0	0	0		ARodriguez 3b	3	0	0	0
Mora dh	4	0	0	0		MStanley lf	3	0	1	0
Belanger ss	4	0	0	0		PGarcia 2b	2	0	0	0
BRobinson 3b	2	0	1	0		Kimm c	3	0	1	0
DDuncan c	3	0	0	0		Fidrych p	0	0	0	0
Cuellar p	0	0	0	0						
Pagan p	0	0	0	0						
Total	30	0	4	0		Total	29	4	7	4

```
BALTIMORE ............................................ 000 000 000—0
DETROIT ............................................. 300 100 00x—4
```

E—Grich. DP—Baltimore 1, Detroit 1. LOB—Baltimore 7, Detroit 3. 2B—A.Johnson, Kimm. HR—Staub (6), J.Thompson (12). SB—LeFlore. S—Blair.

	IP	H	R	ER	BB	SO
Cuellar (L, 4—9)	3⅔	6	4	4	2	0
Pagan	4⅓	1	0	0	0	4
Fidrych (W, 9—1)	9	4	0	0	3	4

WP—Fidrych. T—1:54. A—51,032.

Friday, July 9
VS. KANSAS CITY

Much to the disappointment of 51,041 screaming fans at Tiger Stadium, their prince charming didn't win.

To hear him describe it, The Bird should have gotten clobbered. He told reporters, "Hell, no!" when they asked him if he had pitched well.

"I didn't have any control," The Bird said. "My control was horseshit. I was getting way behind on the hitters and you are not supposed to do that. I screwed it up.

"My parents were here and this was one game I didn't want to lose. I just screwed up."

He screwed up? He lost, 1–0.

It was a tough game, action-packed, with his teammates backing him up in the field but not at the plate.

The Bird gave up a hit to the lead-off batter,

Al Cowens. But Tom Veryzer started a double play on the next man up. And George Brett, the league's leading batter, flied out to end the inning.

In the second, Hal McRae drew a walk—another Fidrych no-no—and he too was wiped out with a double play.

In the fourth inning, the luck ran out.

With one out, The Bird gave up consecutive singles to Brett, John Mayberry, and McRae. The last hit wasn't much—an infield grounder to Veryzer—but the shortstop couldn't make a play. Brett scored.

The Tigers made another double play to get Fidrych out of the inning.

The Bird calmed down and wasn't in trouble again until the last inning. Again his teammates curbed a rally with yet another double play.

But they didn't hit for him.

Dennis Leonard, a pitcher who was every bit as good as Fidrych on this particular night, was making his seventeenth start of the season. Going into the previous season, he had a 20–5 record from Fourth of July to Fourth of July.

There were no "Go, Dennis, go!" chants, no "Leonard for President" bumper stickers, no "Go Dennis!" T-shirts.

But the twenty-five-year-old pitcher wasn't even threatened with a Tiger rally all night long despite the deafening cheers for the other pitcher.

He looked like Fidrych coming down the stretch.

He deserved a good cheer.

But even in defeat, it was The Bird who was acknowledged.

Old-timers at Tiger Stadium could never remember a game when the whole house shook with ovation when the announcement " . . . losing pitcher, Mark Fid—" was made.

If The Bird was ever going to know what a hold he had on Tiger fans, he had to know it this night.

As he was down in the clubhouse, underneath the stands, trying to explain how bad he was, the crowd above him refused to leave. Just plain refused. Tens of thousands of them.

"We want The Bird! We want The Bird! We want The Bird!"

They chanted in that cadence that only politicians hear after they've been nominated for President, or officials hear at civil disorders from angry demonstrators.

But these fans weren't angry.

They wanted to let their hero know that he was still appreciated, even in defeat. He had given them something, now they wanted to give him something back.

Other players may have felt that kind of love after winning a World Series for their team, or on a special day arranged for them when their careers were on the wane.

But a rookie losing pitcher, halfway through his first season . . . ?

For minutes, the fans chanted over and over, "We WANT The Bird!"

They meant it.

Finally, a stadium security man caught The Bird naked and in the midst of a beer run. The security man had a walkie-talkie in his hand that was taking messages from throughout the stands, where other frantic security men felt helpless.

"Mark, you've gotta go out there so we can get these people out of here," he pleaded.

"But I'm undressed," The Bird said. "What am I supposed to do?"

"I've got fifty thousand people out there," he said, and his count was very close to accurate. Just about nobody had left. "They won't leave unless you go out there."

The Bird, for all the adulation he had received in Detroit, couldn't believe him.

"You gotta be kidding me," he said, with a funny grin on his face.

Then he put on a pair of washed-out gray pants and his Tiger jacket over his birthday suit and sprinted to the dugout.

It was now sixteen minutes after the game, and most of the 50,000 were still there. They had been disappointed just before that when a batboy in a Tiger uniform came out, evoking 50,000 cheers, but this time it was for real.

The Bird may have made his greatest move ever by acknowledging his fans in defeat.

The accumulative cheer was rocking the stadium. People in center field who could hardly distinguish his face but knew the curly hair and the enthusiasm, roared. Kids pounded on the top of the dugout with their feet. Dapper men and fashionable women in the box seats clapped and shouted.

Then he returned, as the crowd trickled out, satisfied.

"Right now, I just wish I could be by myself," he told the reporters who awaited his return. "I'd like to think things over."

But he talked to them for another twenty minutes, answering all the questions and trying to give his explanation.

"I'll get them next time," he concluded.

Then he dug through his equipment till he found what he wanted.

"Anybody want a cookie?" he offered.

Sixteen thousand dollars.

That was his salary. It had to be the biggest bargain in baseball for management. In just three games, concluding with the Kansas City loss, he had drawn 149,928 fans to Tiger Stadium. A tenth of the profits on the concessions alone would have paid that salary.

In the state legislature in Lansing, a politician had introduced a resolution asking Tiger general manager Jim Campbell to tear up Fidrych's $16,000 contract for one more fitting with his accomplishments.

The legislator's name was "Angel." In Hell, Michigan, a fan wanted to begin taking up a collection to help the rookie. A Detroit radio station reported getting a dollar from a man in Colorado who had heard of The Bird's low salary.

People in the streets and the newspapers were debating the big question: Should The Bird get more money at midseason, or should he wait till the end of the year to renegotiate his salary?

The lead Letter to the Editor in the Detroit *News* one day came from a fan pleading that he not get an agent. "My kids and I have seen you twice," the man wrote. "Those times were evenings we'll never forget. . . . The world of baseball is slightly a-tilt right now. But, Mark, you can push the reset button. . . . Rewards are nice. . . . Don't get an agent! Be yourself!"

Everyone, including Tiger management, felt he deserved more money. It didn't take a genius to come to that conclusion. And Tiger management had to ponder the question of finding him more money now or taking a chance that some slick agent would get a hold of him and milk the team for all it was worth.

That kind of thinking wasn't selfish. One-twelfth of the players in major-league baseball were playing out their options, many on the advice of agents, to jump their current teams and head for bigger money in places like New York City and Los Angeles.

Everyone was talking money to Fidrych, but the only time he spoke about it was when the subject was brought up.

"If they tore up my contract and wrote a new

one," he told one sportswriter, "it might go to my head. No, sir, I'm happy."

The Tigers made a point of telling people that it was up to them and Fidrych to resolve their financial dealings, not the media or the legislature.

"Don't worry," said John Fetzer. "We're going to look after his welfare, come hell or high water. That's our business."

The Tigers, always a generous team by baseball standards, didn't want to set a precedent of giving new contracts at midseason, much as Fidrych deserved one.

They did pay him an extra $7,500 in bonus money they owed him—and were happy to do it. It was the result of that special clause which was in his contract when he signed with the team originally.

According to that clause, he would be given an additional $1,000 if he spent ninety days on a Class AA minor-league roster, another $1,500 for ninety days on a Class AAA roster, and an additional $5,000 for ninety days on the major-league roster.

The Bird had advanced so fast that he never did stay on the minor-league rosters for the 1976 season. So the Tigers lumped all the bonuses together and presented him with $7,500 just before the Kansas City game.

The week of the Kansas City game, the Ford Dealers of Greater Detroit also presented him with the use of a new Ford Thunderbird, a $10,000 car that got them more than $10,000 in publicity.

But for the most part, Mark Fidrych's earnings were less than some players get for sitting on the bench for the World Series. He was making less than the sanitation men get in a year for cleaning up the messes caused by The Bird's fans outside Tiger Stadium. He got less than the policemen who unsnarled the traffic jams he was causing.

In New York City, Catfish Hunter was making $3.8 million over a long-term contract, and his record fell far short of Fidrych's. That is, his win-loss record and his record for drawing crowds.

The Bird, as would be typical of many twenty-one-year-olds, hardly knew the value of things like endorsements, personal appearances, speaking engagements, or agent's commissions.

To protect him in such matters, the Tigers held a meeting with him one day between the Yankee and Kansas City games.

Hal Middlesworth, the team's director of public relations, and Lew Matlin, a well-traveled and worldly assistant, explained how such things work, and what to watch out for.

An athlete can commit himself deeply if he is as naïve as Fidrych was.

They spoke for about a half hour, and the main thing the Tiger officials tried to impress upon him was not to spend all his time with these people.

To date, Fidrych's endorsements were few. He didn't even get included in the series of bubble-gum cards that proliferate America because he was late being assigned to the Tigers' roster.

He had an offer to help promote a store at a shopping center in suburban Drayton Plains and he took part in a series of autograph-signing appearances at a Detroit pizza outlet called Little Caesar's.

Mostly, however, people were making money off him without his permission, or even without his knowledge. Outside Tiger Stadium, the streets were full of people hawking "Bird" pins, bumper stickers, posters, and T-shirts. They were getting a dollar in some cases for a five-cent item. Some firm wrote and copyrighted a song about him.

Meanwhile, The Bird was having some money problems of his own.

The quick climb to the majors meant that he needed a new car (his '69 Chevy wasn't good enough), some new clothes, a better apartment, some furniture for it, etc.

His father said he was having a slight problem because his auto insurance rate—he was in just about as high a bracket there as one can be—increased when he went to Detroit. His father also said one reason he didn't have a telephone was because of the cost to him right after he moved to Detroit for the season.

A couple of days before the Baltimore game, The Bird was talking about the many letters he was getting, and how he was handling them.

He spoke first about the fact that he didn't know these people who were writing him, and that his replies would be just as meaningless. Then he added:

"Besides, ten times thirteen cents a day for postage is a lot of money."

Teammates were careful about getting caught up in his personal matters, but they could not help.

Relief pitcher John Hiller and outfielder Ron LeFlore, both of whom found instant fame in Detroit, warned him not to open his door to everyone with a briefcase who wanted to get The Bird's name on an endorsement.

Rusty Staub was more explicit.

"He must be attentive to the purpose," said Staub, who has gone through the gamut of promotions in Houston, Montreal, and New York. Staub is a gourmet cook who is constantly getting offers for his menus, cookbooks, etc.

"Certain people on the periphery could destroy him. He doesn't need a Jerry Kapstein [a lawyer-agent who landed some of the biggest players in baseball for his clients] or anything and everything like that. I can't lead his life, but I've offered my help."

Finally, at the suggestion of those close to him, Fidrych signed on with the William Morris Co., one of the most prominent talent agencies in the world. William Morris arranges movie roles, book contracts, television appearances and things of that caliber along with endorsements. The company is always on the lookout for instant stars.

How did they find Fidrych?

Stephen Pinkus of William Morris's New York City office said it was his wife who convinced him what a special personality The Bird was when she was watching a nationally televised game.

"Honey," she said, "come look at him. He is the most adorable thing to come along."

Pinkus, a merchandising executive in William Morris's television division, watched.

"He came across the screen as a real star," Pinkus said.

Pinkus, in describing Fidrych's "star qualities," used such words as "uniqueness" and "electrifying."

"Why do people spend money to watch Barbara Streisand?" he continued. "Or Joe Namath, who made the American Football League? They can't explain, they just do. Mark has the same qualities. He's honest, he enjoys what he does, he does it well. There's nothing phony about him."

William Morris, through Pinkus and Peter Kelly, planned to take a low-profile approach to promoting their new product.

They would not represent him in salary negotiations.

Their first item of importance was to keep people away from him so he could pitch. This, and William Morris's nationally known reputation, is what interested the Tigers in the first place when they brought the company together with Mark and his father, who helped him negotiate their agreement.

The other priority was to get the poor brands that were pirating Fidrych's endorsements—or use of his name—off the market.

"Why should some innocent kid get stuck with a Mark Fidrych baseball cap for $3 or $4, especially if it's garbage?" said Pinkus. "We can go to a big company and get something that won't fall apart. And Mark will get his fair share from it."

Pinkus also said he had a list of almost every television variety show—Mike Douglas, Johnny Carson, others—who wanted Fidrych. But with a talent agency, Fidrych would not have to personally turn such high-powered programs down. William Morris could book him for the off-season, or whenever he became a fully established pitcher. At The Bird's convenience.

And how many twenty-one-year-old baseball players could boast about their agent being the same people who represent Henry Aaron and Secretariat?

GAME PLAYED JULY 9

KANSAS CITY	ab	r	h	bi
Cowens rf	4	0	1	0
Otis cf	4	0	0	0
GBrett 3b	4	1	1	0
Mayberry 1b	4	0	2	0
McRae lf	3	0	3	1
Quirk dh	4	0	0	0
JMartinez c	3	0	1	0
Patek ss	3	0	0	0
FWhite 2b	3	0	1	0
Leonard p	0	0	0	0
Total	32	1	9	1

DETROIT	ab	r	h	bi
LeFlore cf	4	0	0	0
Veryzer ss	4	0	1	0
Oglivie lf	4	0	1	0
Staub rf	4	0	1	0
JThompson 1b	3	0	0	0
ARodriguez 3b	3	0	0	0
PGarcia 2b	2	0	0	0
Meyer ph	1	0	0	0
Wockenfuss c	0	0	0	0
Kimm c	2	0	1	0
MStanley ph	1	0	0	0
Manuel 2b	0	0	0	0
Fidrych p	0	0	0	0
Total	31	0	4	0

```
KANSAS CITY .................................. 000 100 000—1
DETROIT     .................................. 000 000 000—0
```

E—Leonard, G.Brett, Patek, LeFlore. DP—Detroit 4. LOB—Kansas City 5, Detroit 4. 2B—F.White. SB—Oglivie, Staub.

	IP	H	R	ER	BB	SO
Leonard (W, 9–3)	9	4	0	0	0	8
Fidrych (L, 9–2)	9	9	1	1	1	2

T—2:03. A—51,041.

Tuesday, July 13
THE ALL-STAR GAME

If the season to date had been a dream for The Bird, starting the major leagues' forty-seventh All-Star game had to be a fantasy. He had known for a week that he had been chosen to the squad. But he downplayed it at first. "I just want to pitch one inning so I can say that I've played in an All-Star game," he told reporters before going to Philadelphia. "If I start, I start. I just don't want to go and sit the bench."

On the Sunday before the Tuesday game, it was made clear that he wasn't about to sit the bench.

The public-address announcer told the Tiger Stadium crowd just after the start of an afternoon game with the Kansas City Royals that Darrell Johnson, manager of the American League stars, had selected Mark Fidrych to be his starter.

The Bird flew out of the dugout to acknowledge

the fans' universal approval. A wide smile spread across his face. He said, "Wow," and "Wowww" again.

Fidrych had never pitched in an all-star game of any type before—not in the Little Leagues, not in high school, not in the minors.

Only one rookie, Dave Stenhouse of the old Washington Senators, had ever started an All-Star game, and he was twenty-eight years old at the time. Stenhouse pitched the 1962 game after compiling a 10–4 record, and 2.73 earned-run average by midseason. After that, he did virtually nothing in his career, and soon faded away. Nobody made a big deal of his starting assignment and most people forgot about it soon after.

But The Bird would go to Philadelphia as the star of the show, the wunderkind everyone wanted to see.

If he was nervous, he didn't show it when he went out to groom the dirt around the mound and throw his warm-up pitches before an audience of 63,974. It was the largest crowd ever to see a game in Philadelphia, and the third largest to watch an All-Star contest. The game, at Veterans Stadium, was promoted as baseball's contribution to the Bicentennial.

Though he was unruffled, and his fastball hummed at 93 miles per hour according to the TV network's gauge, he didn't pitch well.

The National League, winners of thirteen of the past fourteen such games, had a roster full of hard-hitters who were eager to challenge the American League's well-publicized star. They had heard enough about him and were ready to get a whack at him.

"We won't be standing in the batter's box laughing at him," warned Joe Morgan of the Cincinnati Reds. Morgan had been the National League's Most Valuable Player the previous year.

Pete Rose, Morgan's teammate and a player working on accumulating 3,000 major league hits, was the first man to face The Bird.

Fidrych gave him an outside pitch for an opener, then came back with a high fast one. Rose smacked it past the pitcher's mound and into center field for a single.

When the ball was retrieved, Fidrych took a look at the batter, Steve Garvey of the Los Angeles Dodgers, and turned around to tighten up his defense. He made a motion for them to move to the center and close the infield gap. Then he tried to go to work on Garvey.

The first pitch was a ball, and the second one inside the strike zone, but Garvey sliced it to right field. It fell in front of the lumbering Rusty Staub, then veered past him to the corner of the outfield. Staub stumbled on the well-worn artificial turf as he chased it down, and Rose hustled around the bases to score. Garvey wound up on third with a double.

The crowd was made up mostly of vocal locals, and in Philadelphia, some 50,000 or more of them can be very partisan. The Philadelphia fans are National League boosters, because that is the league the Phillies are in. And in 1976, there was more reason than ever to cheer. The Phillies were more than ten games in front of the runner-up in their division, and hopefully on their way to their first pennant since 1950.

Several of the hard-hitting Phillies were on the National League squad, so naturally the Nationals were adopted as the home team in this game.

Mark Fidrych was just some illusion, some American League upstart as far as the crowd was concerned. He was fast becoming a delusion.

He was in trouble.

He stalked a bit, then got back to the business at hand and went after Joe Morgan on the first pitch. Morgan popped to right field, and it took a strong throw by Staub to save another run.

Fidrych got George Foster, another hard-hitting Cincinnati player, out on a grounder on his second pitch, but Garvey scored in the process. Then The Bird ended the disastrous inning by getting Greg Luzinski of the Phillies to pop to first base.

Fidrych threw even faster in the second inning, letting go of the ball as if it were a hot potato.

He threw five pitches to Johnny Bench, the feared catcher of the Reds, in less than 60 seconds. The incredible rah-tah-tah was to no avail, however. Bench lashed the last of those pitches for a single.

After The Bird got Dave Kingman, the New York Met who led the majors in homers, on a pop-up, Dave Concepcion of the Reds sent a screaming single under Fidrych's feet.

The Bird was in trouble again.

But he retired Randy Jones, the National League pitcher, on a strikeout. And he was talking up a storm as he met Rose for a second time. He seemed like he was getting his act together.

He got Rose on an infield out, and was out of the inning.

He was also out of the game.

With Fidrych due at bat to lead off the third inning for the American League, Darrell Johnson lifted him for a pinch-hitter, an obvious move.

He was sent to the showers, the eventual losing pitcher in the American League's 7–1 defeat. He didn't return to his favorite far corner of the dugout to cheer his new teammates on. This game was clearly different, not only a defeat but in some ways a resounding one.

The Bird threw only twenty-one pitches to ten batters in the All-Star game. It was as if he wanted to get out of Philadelphia in a hurry.

And no wonder that he did.

The reason for wanting out was not the usual one people joke about when they visit Philadelphia—you know, "I went to Philadelphia but it was closed," or, "I spent a week in Philadelphia one Sunday."

No, The Bird's reason was totally to the contrary. Life in Philly was just too fast for him.

He was pressured more than at any other time in

his short major-league career. About forty hours
of the fastest pace he'd ever been involved in.
Everybody—fans, writers, broadcasters, photographers, promoters, even the opposing players—
wanted a piece of him. From the way he pitched,
fast but ingloriously, he seemed to buckle.

An All-Star pitcher is allowed only three innings if he is a starter. That's not much time to
make up a 2–0 deficit. It's not much time to learn
about nine other batters who you haven't faced before, or become accustomed to a new catcher.

But mainly the pressure of the media stole away
his key athletic strength—his concentration. This
may have been one game where he should have
stopped and had a good talk with the ball, then
pointed it in the right direction for a moment before throwing it.

By game time, that was probably too late. The
two days of hoopla had usurped that concentration.

While The Bird had to cater to only a dozen or
so reporters in Detroit or on road trips around the
American League, he had to face two hundred in
Philadelphia. Tough, seasoned reporters who
wouldn't shy away when Fidrych went into his
spiel about baseball's being a job, an eight-hour-
a-day job at that.

The Bird has this way about him when he deals
with reporters, and it works. He handles the pressures of interviews by turning his back on them
when he wants to finish. He's natural about it, not

rude. But he can chop his sentences in half, re-
fuse to comment on hardly anything in depth, and
sometimes begins talking about something completely different from what he was asked.

It's kind of a flighty mannerism, and it comes
off as a subconscious defense mechanism. He
doesn't seem to do it by design, and therefore reporters aren't offended. He just can't be pinned
down. He tries to be helpful to a point, but he
can't stay in one place too long.

But every time he turned away from a group of
reporters in Philadelphia, he bumped into another
group behind him. And they had a set of the same
questions they wanted answered first-hand.

The writers were sent to Philadelphia to get
"the" story, and that story was The Bird.

The photographers were even worse. They
shouted, they pushed, they demanded "just one
more photo, Mark." When they got it, they would
ask, "How about one more?"

There were the magazine people, the network
radio men shoving microphones in his face, the
television people trying to grab him off to the
side for film.

There were people from important publications
—*The New York Times, Sports Illustrated,* national
television—who just weren't used to being turned
down.

They all seemed to be saying in unison, "Hey,
Mark, we need some of your time."

Fidrych, after taking a Sunday night off to go

to an Elton John concert in Pontiac, Michigan, got up at 6:30 Monday morning to fly to Philadelphia. Being a late riser, that was hard enough.

But there was no peace and quiet for him until game time, and with most of the 63,974 people rooting against him, there wasn't much peace of mind then, either.

From his arrival at Philadelphia, where he quickly whisked to his hotel and the ballpark, there was a steady stream of interruptions.

The floodgates were opened once he arrived in town, and everybody needed something exclusive.

He missed breakfast. He missed lunch. Besides interviewers, there were autograph hounds.

"Can't you take just a minute to . . .?" they'd ask.

"But I'm hungry, and . . ." he tried to answer.

And then the pressure would build up. *Sports Illustrated*'s guy, who wanted a picture of him in street clothes, made it clear he was from SI, the guy frow KYW television made it clear he was with the *Mike Douglas Show,* and others would change their tunes from "want" to "need."

The more he accommodated, the more they needed or wanted.

They all knew they could bend the head of this neophyte, so they did. Fidrych went along with just about every wish the media had.

It was bedlam.

About the only break The Bird got that day came when he had to speak at the scheduled news conference at the Bellvue Stratford Hotel. At least in the ballroom, he would be at the podium where they couldn't crowd him, or make their individual demands.

It's safe to say that Fidrych stole the show there —by being himself.

He wasn't the only star subject. Randy Jones, the San Diego pitcher who was assigned to start for the National League, was also present. So were George Brett, the American League's leading batter, and the opposing managers and a couple of Hall of Famers—Robin Roberts and Bob Lemon— who had been given dignitary status as honorary captains.

But the crowd of about two hundred newsmen had come to hear The Bird.

Joe Falls of the Detroit *Free Press* wrote of the gathering:

"It was unbelievable. No player ever took this kind of hold on the media in the All Star setting and what was so beautiful is that Fidrych had nothing to do with it. They told him to show up and he did, and he just talked. The best he could. With his hands. With his arms. With his eyes. With his hair. And with his heart, you know."

He was introduced as "a young man who really needs no introduction," and everybody applauded.

He began his talk by fishing for words—a few "ah . . . geez . . . er . . . I" warm-ups—then conceded and asked: "What do you want me to say?"

There was some fiddling with the microphone to make it work, and finally someone popped up, "Say something, Mark."

He did. "It's the thrill of a lifetime to be here."

As the writers made note of his comment, he asked them: "How was that?"

The place broke up in laughter.

Baseball figures are no different from political figures. The writers will take down everything they say, and laugh at any halfway joke. Maybe it's because the public figures—be they athletes or politicos—make the writers' jobs easier with their ready-made interviews. Nothing really new comes out of such joint interview sessions, but a lot of newspaper space is eaten up and a lot of radio time logged.

Nothing deep, nothing provocative, nothing hardly newsworthy. But Fidrych continued, and reporters applauded, laughed and scribbled it all down.

He stood before them decked out in a pair of dungarees and a print shirt. "They didn't tell me I had to wear leisure suits," he said before leaving Detroit. He looked, and was, very natural as he proceeded.

They wanted to know anything about this new star. "Do you consider yourself kooky?" "What do you say to the ball?" "What do you do in your spare time?"

The Bird gave them answers to fit the down-home, raw-rookie image they had conjured up through tales that passed from sportswriter to sportswriter.

He told them the most exciting thing that ever happened to him before this day was "When I bought a mini-bike when I was fourteen." He told them that if he wasn't in baseball, he'd be working at the garage in Northboro. He told them that in his spare time he liked to work on his car, go fishing, go out with girls.

And when he was asked if there was anything that could top all this, he said: "Getting married."

Finally, the braver but more inane questions were popped at him.

"Mark, is it true that you used to like to watch butterflies?"

The Bird looked at the questioner. He was befuddled.

"What do you mean? I don't understand the question."

The reporter repeated himself: "Is it true that you used to spend your time watching butterflies?"

That was just a little too much for the patient Fidrych.

"No, I never watched butterflies. No, no, I never did that. Bye-bye. It was nice meeting you."

And he left, still wondering about that last question.

Somehow, from all that and the questions asked before the group interview, stories got written and the legend grew.

A Philadelphia writer reported that Fidrych's public speaking "is three parts frenzy, one part anarchy and two parts 33-rpm record being played at 78 rpm."

Another Philadelphia writer concluded: "He may be the last American innocent and he is more fun than anybody else in the major leagues."

The New York Times's representative wrote: "In this era of 'freedom,' Mark Fidrych is a rags-to-riches story. He has captivated audiences more with his style than with his success."

From the Atlantic to the Pacific, the word about The Bird was passed.

About the only thing new that was learned about The Bird, however, was from an enterprising Long Island reporter who observed that Fidrych squirted a can of deodorant at his street socks after he undressed and put on his uniform for a workout. The same reporter noticed that Fidrych's two pair of baseball spikes included three shoes for the right foot and one for the left.

The pressures continued right up until game time, and for the pre-game finale, there was a visit from the President of the United States.

Gerald Ford visited both teams just before they took the field.

When Presidents get chummy at sports events, there's almost always an ulterior motive. The last time a President saw one of these games was in 1969, when Richard Nixon was in the White House and the game was in Washington.

Baseball was celebrating its one-hundredth birthday and Mr. Nixon decided to throw a bash for the sportswriters in the East Room at the White House. The President was not having much luck on the front pages that summer, so he tried for the sports page.

He told all the journalists who assembled about how it was when he was a boy in 1929 and listened to the World Series. He proceeded to recall the details.

That was nice, except that he had had his aides scurry about earlier that day to learn all the details they could about the 1929 World Series.

Gerald Ford was out for bigger stakes, which is why he wasted little time getting over to meet The Bird.

The President knew the All-Star game that night was one thing that could compete with the National Democratic Convention in New York City for television viewers. The Democrats had scheduled Jimmy Carter to present his platform, a highlight that they wanted to go national with in order to gain voter support.

When President Ford entered the American League dressing room, there was a big commotion.

Good old company man Mark, the 9-to-5 baseball man, looked up and remarked: "I thought we had a game to play."

But the President was determined to meet The Bird as he went down the makeshift reception line.

"You're The Bird! How are you?" he said, sincerely excited about meeting him. The President jabbed a finger at him when he met him.

Mark looked up and asked bluntly: "Did you send me a thing in Texas?"

Ron LeFlore, sitting next to Fidrych, mentioned

that The Bird got the "thing"—a congratulatory message supposedly from Ford—in Baltimore, not Texas.

"I tried to call you," said the President.

As it turned out, the telegram he got in Baltimore was signed by Gerald Ford, but sent by his teammates.

The conversation continued between two of the most famous men in America with The Bird asking about the President's son, Jack.

The President was more interested in talking about himself, and told The Bird that: "Now don't talk to those young fellows, talk to the old man."

"Oh, okay," said The Bird. "I just was wondering how he was doing with those dates."

The President laughed.

"Come to Washington and he'll fix you up."

"I may do that."

It was Fidrych's highlight of the day. He came close to asking the President of the United States to help him get fixed up with Chris Evert, the tennis star who dated the President's son.

The President achieved his goal of mingling with the young, and knocking the Democrats out of the box in the television scores. In Detroit alone, informal polls showed Fidrych and the game drawing about 80 to 90 percent of the television audience. The Democrats split the rest with movie reruns. Nationally, about 75 million people watched the game.

But the distractions didn't help Fidrych's pitching.

He hurled his worst game of the season.

In his own mind, however, The Bird came out ahead.

"It's the biggest thrill of my life," he said. "Up until now, the biggest thrill that's happened to me was nothing."

ALL-STAR GAME (PLAYED JULY 13)

AMERICAN	ab	r	h	bi	NATIONAL	ab	r	h	bi
LeFlore lf	2	0	1	0	Rose 3b	3	1	2	0
Yastrmski 1b	2	0	0	0	Oliver lf	1	0	0	0
Carew 1b	3	0	0	0	Garvey 1b	3	1	1	1
Brett 3b	2	0	0	0	Cash 2b	1	1	1	0
Money 3b	1	0	0	0	Morgan 2b	3	1	1	0
Munson c	2	0	0	0	Perez 1b	0	0	0	0
Fisk c	1	0	0	0	Foster rf	3	1	1	3
Chambliss ph	1	0	0	0	Mntefusco p	0	0	0	0
Lynn cf	3	1	1	1	Russel ss	1	0	0	0
Otis ph	1	0	0	0	Luzinski lf	3	0	0	0
Harrah ss	2	0	0	0	Griffey rf	1	1	1	1
Belanger ss	1	0	0	0	Bench c	2	0	1	0
Patek ss	0	0	0	0	Cedeno rf	2	1	1	2
Staub rf	2	0	2	0	Kingman rf	2	0	0	0
Tiant p	0	0	0	0	Boone c	2	0	0	0
Wynegar ph	0	0	0	0	Concpcion ss	2	0	1	0
Tanana p	0	0	0	0	Bowa ss	1	0	0	0
Grich 2b	2	0	0	0	Rhoden p	0	0	0	0
Garner 2b	1	0	0	0	Cey 3b	0	0	0	0
Fidrych p	0	0	0	0	Jones p	1	0	0	0
McRae ph	1	0	0	0	Seaver p	1	0	0	0
Hunter p	0	0	0	0	Schmidt 3b	1	0	0	0
Rivers rf	2	0	1	0	Forsch p	0	0	0	0
Total	29	1	5	1	Total	33	7	10	7

AMERICAN	....	000 100 000—1
NATIONAL	....	202 000 03x—7

DP—American 1, National 3. LOB—American 4, National 3. 3B—Garvey, Rose. HR—Foster (1), Lynn (1), Cedeno (1). SB—Carew.

	IP	H	R	ER	BB	SO
Fidrych (L, 0–1)	2	4	2	2	0	1
Hunter	2	2	2	2	0	3
Tiant	2	1	0	0	0	1
Tanana	2	3	3	3	1	0
Jones (W, 1–0)	3	2	0	0	1	1
Seaver	2	2	1	1	0	1
Montefusco	2	0	0	0	2	2
Rhoden	1	1	0	0	0	0
Forsch	1	0	0	0	0	1

PB—Munson. T—2:15. A—63,974.

Friday, July 16
VS. OAKLAND

After the mediocre All-Star showing, a very definite question arose: Had The Bird phenomenon finally run its course?

The next pitching assignment came just three days after the National League hitters had batted a little sense about reality into The Bird's head. Forget the reality. At Tiger Stadium for Fidrych's next start, 45,905 fans showed up to revive the fantasy.

The Bird didn't let them down.

They were screaming fans again, chanting the omnipresent "Go, Bird, go!" to get his juices flowing every time a clutch situation arose. The sign carriers were here in force. "Sit on it, Fonz. Mark is NO. 1" was the best of the night. And there was a new dimension of Birdomania as a small plane pulled a banner around the stadium several times.

It read: "Happy Birthday Melody Farms"—whatever that meant.

What did make sense was that thousands of fans he had captured were still with him. It was a homecoming in which they deserved one of his better efforts, and he gave it to them.

Oakland was a solid team, full of stars, and was one of only two American League teams which The Bird had not beaten yet (Chicago was the other). He had pitched to one batter in his relief role in April when he made his major-league debut, but that was all.

The first man up, speedy Bill North, slapped a single into left field. With Billy Williams at bat, North tried to steal. Catcher Bruce Kimm made a strong throw to Pedro Garcia at second base to nail North.

Williams walked. Fidrych turned and gave his second-base combination some words of encouragement, as if to rev them up. The next batter was Don Baylor, a heavy hitter who was the only player Fidrych faced the first time he pitched against Oakland. Baylor was the player Fidrych called "lucky" after he got a hit off him.

But Fidrych's hopeful words to his second-base combination seemed to do more good than his brash remark to Baylor a couple of months back. The next pitch after Fidrych had revved up his teammates, they came through with a double-play —from short to second to first.

That livened up The Bird.

For the next five innings, he put the A's down

in order. The Tiger infield especially was making some great plays behind him. Sixteen of eighteen A's outs were infield outs.

For much of that time, Tiger fans had been relatively subdued except for their pre-game ovations for The Bird. The Tigers themselves had been listless at bat, going out with the same regularity that Fidrych was mowing down the A's. The first eighteen Tigers to go to bat made out: two of them had gotten on base with hits but were out after errant base running.

An incident in the sixth inning, however, aroused the crowd and got it wildly behind The Bird.

Claudell Washington was the lead-off batter for the A's and he decided to test The Bird's patience. Washington fussed and fidgeted before stepping into the batter's box, hoping that The Bird would fume. It was a long, long delay. After the game, Oakland manager Chuck Tanner would say that Washington supposedly had been told by Amos Otis of the Kansas City Royals that this was one way to get to The Bird.

While Washington was stalling, The Bird did a few of his exercises, then went into a squat on the mound while waiting for him. The first pitch was a strike.

Washington delayed again. This time, The Bird was trying to regain his concentration and thrust his right arm out with the ball in it and aimed it at the plate. His index finger was out as he jiggled his wrist to make himself loose.

Washington, who had never seen The Bird

pitch before, apparently thought Fidrych was pointing at him. When The Bird came in with a low inside pitch on his next throw, Washington thought Fidrych had tried to throw at him. After all, here was the young pitcher who supposedly could put the ball wherever he wanted to.

Washington took a few steps toward the mound, his bat in hand.

Ye Gods, Washington versus The Bird, the Tigers and 45,000 fans.

Suddenly the field became full of players. Tiger pitchers came all the way from the left-field bullpen to bolster the ranks of Fidrych's defenders. The stands looked as though they might overspill onto the field if Washington really did take on The Bird.

It was tense.

Bruce Kimm followed Washington to restrain him. Enough players and umpires got into peacemaking roles and a riot was averted, but the Tiger fans went crazy with the booing. They wouldn't let up.

The Bird later explained, and it made sense, that he wasn't about to hit the lead-off batter in a 0–0 game. And he proved that all he wanted was an out when he got Washington on the next pitch to ground out.

Washington couldn't take a step after that without being booed loudly.

The incident not only brought the fans to life, it kept them there.

The "Go, Bird, go!" chants began, and The Bird

responded by throwing strikes one after the other. The Bird was all hyper now. On a foul ball, he rushed in and picked up Kimm's mask and handed it to him.

This was The Bird that 45,000 fans had come to see.

In the next inning, the A's got three men on base. It didn't matter. They didn't score. With two out, The Bird got his first strikeout of the game—against Sal Bando, the American League's leading home-run hitter. The fans went berserk.

In the eighth inning, the A's got two men on. They didn't score either. "Go, Bird, go!" The fans were going nuts.

The Tigers remained scoreless and the game went into extra innings. Things were tense because Detroit was getting no hits at all and the A's were getting closer with Fidrych. The A's were putting base runners on in each inning.

But The Bird was throwing strikes when things got tough. And the fans were really with him. In the eleventh inning, he was on the mound pumping the ball before he threw it, pointing the ball for precision throws, bouncing it off his palm.

The A's got two men on in the eleventh after one was out. And Oakland's coach had a long conference with Bill North, one of the base runners, in an attempt to rattle Fidrych.

But The Bird came back to strike out Baylor, the fifth straight time he put down the player he once called "lucky."

After a short meeting on the mound with man-

ager Ralph Houk, evoking the fans to scream
"leave him in," The Bird got Joe Rudi to fly out.

In the bottom of the eleventh, the Tigers pushed
across a run on Willie Horton's single. Tiger Stadium was the same old noisy, joyous place that
Fidrych was used to.

Nobody left. The hordes of fans demanded his
encore and got it. The homecoming was complete.

As most of the fans trickled out of the exits and
headed for home, cars full of kids rode up and
down Michigan Avenue, yelling and screaming
like it was a high school football victory. The phenomenon was not about to end.

Nor would it end in the coming weeks.

When *Sports Illustrated* did its story on The
Bird, it had Randy Jones, the San Diego pitcher
who started the All-Star game for the National
League, on its cover. The story on Jones empha-
sized how big a drawing card he was: "In his first
dozen appearances at San Diego Stadium this season, he attracted crowds averaging 32,775. . . ."

Big Deal. Jones was an established star going in
to the 1970 season. The Bird, starting from scratch
as a completely unknown entity, was now averaging 34,353 after seven home games.

At home or on the road, The Bird was the biggest thing in baseball.

After sixteen games, home and away, he would
put more than half a million fans in the stands. A
half million. That's halfway home to a good full-
season draw by most teams.

In August, The Bird was still packing them in around the league. One week, when he drew 44,000 to a game in New York City, Randy Jones drew 2,715 in Atlanta. The Bird had eleven victories going into his game that week, Randy Jones had eighteen.

Sports Illustrated concluded its story on Jones by quoting a San Diego sports editor: "This town never before had a figure like Randy Jones." The SI writer had an addendum: "Nor . . . has any other city." There are many who would question that.

Ralph Houk, who had been around major-league baseball for a quarter of a century, had his own version of the impact Fidrych made. Houk had managed Roger Maris the year Maris drew record crowds while breaking Babe Ruth's home-run record. He also managed Mickey Mantle, who had a magnetic hold on crowds.

"Maris got the same kind of reaction from the press [that Fidrych was getting] but he didn't turn the town on the way this boy has," said Houk. "Mantle used to draw the crowds too, but I never saw anything like this."

In the weeks that followed the Oakland homecoming game, The Bird remained the talk of Detroit. Hardly a newspaper went to press that didn't have his name in it. Hardly a disc jockey went on the air without bringing up his name. One disc jockey introduced a godawful song entitled "The Bird."

Around the league, it was incredible too.

In Baltimore, a little old lady leaned over the

dugout roof and asked the Oriole's Reggie Jackson to get Fidrych's autograph on a baseball cap for her.

"Look at this," Jackson said. "A two-hundred-and-fifty-thousand-dollar All-Star like me getting an autograph from The Bird." He laughed and shook his head. In New York, a hungry young reporter waited outside The Bird's room at the Hotel Roosevelt for two hours, to get an interview. Girls actually followed Fidrych onto the team bus after one game. Back in Southgate, Michigan, where his apartment is, the biggest thing to happen in that suburb in some time was when The Bird went to a hairstylist to get his locks cut. Girls were grabbing at the hair before it hit the floor and the local news made the story and photo front-page stuff.

"I've never seen anything like this in my life," said Dick Tracewski, a Tiger coach. "I played with Denny McLain [the former Tiger who won thirty-one games in 1968] and I roomed with Sandy Koufax (the youngest pitcher ever elected to the Hall of Fame) for three years when he was striking out everybody and winning all those games. But nothing like this ever happened."

There still is a question of just how good Fidrych was as he pitched his way into the second half of the season. Scores of young pitchers had failed the test of pitching well against a team the second time around. Pitchers are often fast starters because they have the edge on batters when neither party knows the other. But the second time is the true test.

Sal Bando, the home-run-hitting Oakland player, was assessing Fidrych's talents after the 1–0 defeat The Bird had inflicted on his team. "He has a better idea of what's going on than most pitchers. He's got more maturity than most guys. He's not only different but he's an outstanding pitcher."

But when Bando added, "We still have to see, though. We have a saying in the majors [about rookie pitchers]: What goes around, comes around."

The other question is whether The Bird would remain the same hyped up, enthused player whose personal antics had attracted people to him as much as his pitching.

Vida Blue, an Oakland pitcher who had drawn huge, noisy crowds when he won twenty-four games at age twenty-two, learned to hate the adulation.

But he thought The Bird was different.

"He seems to enjoy the attention—I didn't," said Blue. "He'll make it because people think he's crazy. People knew I was serious."

Blue also said that The Bird would have to learn to handle situations like being bothered at restaurants for autographs and greetings from well-wishers.

Not long after Blue made his remarks, The Bird had one such experience. His reaction was, "I don't mind going to a restaurant and signing a few autographs. The other night I went off to eat in Detroit and I signed autographs the whole meal. But you know what the payoff was? You know what it was, man? The restaurant manager came over and said that I don't have to pay for anything.

"That's not bad, is it?"

GAME PLAYED JULY 16

OAKLAND	ab	r	h	bi	DETROIT	ab	r	h	bi
North cf	5	0	3	0	LeFlore cf	5	1	2	0
MAlexander pr	0	0	0	0	Veryzer ss	3	0	0	0
Haney c	0	0	0	0	Staub rf	3	0	1	0
BWilliams dh	1	0	0	0	Horton dh	5	0	1	1
Lintz pr	0	0	0	0	JThompson 1b	4	0	0	0
McMullen dh	1	0	0	0	AJohnson lf	3	0	1	0
Baylor rf	5	0	0	0	ARodriguez 3b	4	0	1	0
Rudi lf	5	0	2	0	PGarcia 2b	3	0	1	0
Bando 3b	4	0	0	0	Oglivie ph	1	0	0	0
Tenace 1b	4	0	0	0	Wockenfuss c	0	0	0	0
CWashingtn cf	4	0	1	0	Kimm c	3	0	0	0
Garner 2b	4	0	1	0	Meyer ph	1	0	0	0
Sandt ss	3	0	0	0	Scrivener 2b	0	0	0	0
MTorrez p	0	0	0	0	Fidrych p	0	0	0	0
Fingers p	0	0	0	0					
Total	36	0	7	0	Total	35	1	7	1

One out when winning run scored.

OAKLAND	....	000 000 000 00—0
DETROIT	....	000 000 000 01—1

E—C.Washington, Wockenfuss. DP—Detroit 2. LOB—Oakland 7, Detroit 8. 2B—A.Rodriguez. 3B—Staub. SB—M.Alexander. S—Veryzer 2.

	IP	H	R	ER	BB	SO
M.Torrez	8	5	0	0	0	3
Fingers (L, 5—6)	2⅓	2	1	1	2	1
Fidrych (W, 10—2)	11	7	0	0	4	5

HBP—by M.Torrez, (A.Johnson). T—2:26. A—45,905.

GAME PLAYED JULY 20

DETROIT	ab	r	h	bi
LeFlore cf	4	2	2	2
Veryzer ss	4	2	2	0
Staub rf	4	1	3	4
Horton dh	5	0	0	0
JThompson 1b	5	1	2	1
Oglivie lf	2	0	0	0
AJohnson ph	1	0	0	0
MStanley lf	1	0	1	0
ARodriguez 3b	5	0	1	1
PGarcia 2b	4	0	0	0
Kimm c	4	2	3	0
Fidrych p	0	0	0	0
Total	**39**	**8**	**14**	**8**

MINNESOTA	ab	r	h	bi
Braun lf	5	0	2	1
Smalley ss	3	0	1	0
Carew 1b	4	0	0	1
Wynegar c	4	0	1	0
Bostock cf	4	1	1	0
Cubbage 3b	4	0	1	0
Hisle rf	3	1	0	0
Oliva dh	4	1	4	1
Randall 2b	3	0	0	0
Singer p	0	0	0	0
WCampbell p	0	0	0	0
Burgmeir p	0	0	0	0
JHughes p	0	0	0	0
Total	**34**	**3**	**10**	**3**

```
DETROIT    ................................  000 004 310—8
MINNESOTA  ................................  002 100 000—3
```

E—Carew, Wynegar, P.Garcia. DP—Detroit 3, Minnesota 1. LOB—Detroit 8, Minnesota 7. 2B—J.Thompson, Kimm. HR—Staub (7), LeFlore (3). SB—Bostock. S—Randall. SF—Staub.

	IP	H	R	ER	BB	SO
Fidrych (W, 11—2)	9	10	3	3	2	2
Singer (L, 8—6)	6	7	4	4	1	4
W.Campbell	0	3	3	3	0	0
Burgmeir	1	2	0	0	0	1
J.Hughes	2	2	1	1	2	0

T—2:39. A—30,425.

GAME PLAYED JULY 24

DETROIT	ab	r	h	bi	CLEVELAND	ab	r	h	bi
LeFlore cf	3	2	0	0	Lowenstin rf	3	1	1	0
Veryzer ss	5	1	3	1	Spikes rf	2	0	0	0
Staub rf	3	0	1	1	Duffy ss	5	0	0	0
Horton dh	4	0	1	1	Manning cf	5	1	2	0
AJohnson dh	1	0	0	0	Carty dh	4	1	2	0
JThompson 1b	4	1	1	1	Hendrick lf	3	1	2	2
Oglivie lf	3	1	1	1	JPowell 1b	4	0	3	0
ARodriguez 3b	4	0	0	0	BBell 3b	4	0	1	0
PGarcia 2b	3	0	0	0	Fosse c	4	0	1	0
Kimm c	3	0	2	0	TSmith pr	0	0	0	0
Fidrych p	0	0	0	0	Ashby c	0	0	0	0
Hiller p	0	0	0	0	Kuiper 2b	3	0	2	0
					Blanks 2b	1	0	0	0
					JBrown p	0	0	0	0
					Hood p	0	0	0	0
					Kern p	0	0	0	0
					LaRoche p	0	0	0	0
Total	33	5	9	5	Total	38	4	14	2

```
DETROIT    ..................................................  111 100 010—5
CLEVELAND  ..................................................  000 220 000—4
```

E—Bell, Staub, Kimm. DP—Detroit 2, Cleveland 2. LOB—Detroit 8, Cleveland 9. 2B—Horton, Manning. HR—J.Thompson (14), Oglivie (7). SB—Manning, LeFlore. S—Kimm.

	IP	H	R	ER	BB	SO
Fidrych	4⅓	9	4	4	1	2
Hiller (W, 9—4)	4⅔	5	0	0	1	1
J.Brown	4	7	4	4	3	1
Hood	1⅓	0	0	0	1	0
Kern (L, 6—3)	3	2	1	1	2	4
LaRoche	⅔	0	0	0	0	0

T—2:54. A—37,504.

Epilogue

Back in Northboro, where it all started, Mrs. Fidrych ran into Mrs. Pierce at Bill Lowell's Meat Market when Birdomania was at its peak.

The Pierces' own the garage where The Bird used to pump gas. That's probably where he'd be working if he hadn't made it in professional baseball.

"When you see Markie," said Mrs. Pierce, "tell him not to change. Don't ever change."

Then they both had a good cry.

BESTSELLERS
FROM DELL

fiction

non-fiction